PROJECT
MANAGEMENT

Kaplan MBA Fundamentals Series

MBA Fundamentals Business Law

MBA Fundamentals Statistics

MBA Fundamentals Business Writing

MBA Fundamentals Project Management

From the #1 graduate test prep provider, Kaplan MBA Fundamentals helps you to master core business basics in a few easy steps. Each book in the series is based on an actual MBA course, providing direct and measurable skills you can use today.

For the latest titles in the series, as well as downloadable resources, visit:
www.kaplanmbafundamentals.com

MBA
FUNDAMENTALS

PROJECT
MANAGEMENT

Vijay Kanabar, PMP, PhD and
Roger D. Warburton, PMP, PhD

KAPLAN

PUBLISHING

New York

To Dina and Eileen

* * *

© 2008 Vijay Kanabar and Roger D. H. Warburton

Published by Kaplan Publishing, a division of Kaplan, Inc.
1 Liberty Plaza, 24th Floor
New York, NY 10006

Printed in the United States of America

September 2008
10 9 8 7 6 5 4 3 2

ISBN-13: 978-1-4277-9744-5

Kaplan Publishing books are available at special quantity discounts to use for sales promotions, employee premiums, or educational purposes. Please email our Special Sales Department to order or for more information at kaplanpublishing@kaplan.com, or write to Kaplan Publishing, 1 Liberty Plaza, 24th Floor, New York, NY 10006.

Table of Contents

Introduction

This book is intended as a comprehensive introduction for professionals who wish to learn project management at their own pace and on their own schedule. We introduce you to the world of project management and explain what you will need to know to complete a successful project. The content has been developed and polished in introductory and advanced project management courses that we have taught for many years, and our goal is to make the fundamental concepts clear and immediately useful.

This is a great time to study project management, as the discipline of project management and the need for project managers is growing explosively. The Project Management Institute (PMI) has already awarded almost 500,000 Project Management Professional certifications, but the forecasted demand for professionally trained project managers over the next 20 years is over 15 million! PMI has codified the knowledge, skills, and techniques of project management into a professional discipline, which is documented in the Project Management Body of Knowledge (PMBOK), now a global standard. We closely follow the PMBOK in this book, so that the knowledge you acquire will serve you well for many years to come. Since we have taken a "fundamentals" approach, you will find the content relevant even if your interest is in other standards such as Prince 2, or if you use other company-owned proprietary processes.

Projects are undertaken to provide a unique result or service, and have a distinct beginning and end. Projects are becoming more important to governments, non-profit institutions, as well as the business world, as more and more organizations rely on the completion of projects to be successful. Projects today may involve just a single person or many thousands, and may last from a few weeks to several years.

The book is divided into two parts. In part 1, we explain the project management life cycle: Initiating, Planning, Monitoring and Controlling, and Closing. Throughout the book, we analyze real-world cases, which grounds the content in practical, useful methods. Part 2 covers the key skills and tools in the project manager's arsenal: managing communications, cost, risk, and quality, as well as detailed techniques for determining whether your project is under or over budget, and behind or on schedule.

Each chapter has exercises for you to complete with answers provided in Appendix A. We recommend that you steadily work through each exercise. The questions are designed to help you understand the material and are variations on those we have successfully used in introductory project management courses. With the availability of modern project management software, the technical tools for managing projects have become much more accessible. Even small projects can now benefit from inexpensive, automated tools.

PART 1

Introduction to Project Management

INTRODUCTION

What is a project? Whether you are cooking a unique meal, building a boat, planning a 50th wedding anniversary for your parents, or upgrading your operating system, you are engaged in a project. A historical review of Webster's dictionary for the word *project* reveals that this term has evolved from simply being defined as "an idea" in 1910 to a "planned undertaking" today. In today's competitive business world, an idea must be studied and acted upon quickly. Largely due to the maturity of the project management discipline, today a project idea can be quickly planned, executed, and turned into successful results.

WHAT'S AHEAD

- Differentiating between project, operation, and program
- Project management and project life cycle
- The role of project manager
- The skills that a project manager must have
- The role of a project management office

IN THE REAL WORLD

Dunkin' Donuts recently completed a major project to introduce a "zero grams trans fat" menu nationwide. This was a secretive project that was conceived in 2003 and ended in 2007, and apparently only five people in the entire company knew about it. The project team was small and they worked at Dunkin' Donuts's research lab trying to create a recipe for a donut without trans fats that tasted just like those on which the chain had built its reputation over the last half century. This case is a real-world example of project management in action. A unique, well-defined deliverable of strategic importance to a company is produced within a finite amount of time.

KEY CONCEPTS

Projects are typically associated with both *large and small undertakings*. Such initiatives are innovative and complex and require a structured methodology to deliver results. This is what project management is all about. A project produces one or more deliverables. A deliverable is the product or service requested by the authorizing party.

For our purposes, we will define a project as an agreement to deliver specified goods or services within a fixed schedule and for a stipulated amount of money. Furthermore, the importance of clearly defining the scope of goods or services being delivered cannot be understated. Confusion surrounding the scope of the project is possibly the key reason why projects fail.

Projects exist in every organization and vary in scope and magnitude. Some projects may involve one or two resources. Larger projects, such as the construction of a tunnel, involve several organizations all working toward a common goal.

What Do All Projects Have in Common?

All projects share three common characteristics:

1. Projects are temporary; they have a distinct beginning and end.
2. Projects are undertaken to provide a unique result or service known as the deliverable.

3. Projects are developed by breaking them down into smaller steps or stages (progressive elaboration).

PROJECTS VERSUS OPERATIONAL WORK

A common question to consider when defining projects is whether the work should be categorized as a new project or as operational work, especially since both types of work involve similar stages—planning, organizing, executing, and controlling. The purpose of a project is to reach its stated goal and then terminate. But consider the case of a bakery baking bread. Since this is an ongoing, repetitive process day after day, with no distinct beginning or ending, one can classify baking bread as operational work. But if you are attempting to introduce a new flavor of bread or one with reduced sugar, you may want to apply the principles of project management. The Dunkin' Donuts case study introduced at the start of this chapter represents such a project. Once the new recipe has been created, the process of making donuts is categorized as operational work.

PROJECT MANAGEMENT

What is project management? Project management is both an art and a science. It is an art because a talented and experienced project manager is

Figure 1.1 Dunkin' Donuts Press Release

About Us

Dunkin' Donuts Press Room

Press Releases

DUNKIN' DONUTS ANNOUNCES ZERO GRAMS TRANS FAT MENU TO BE AVAILABLE NATIONWIDE BY OCTOBER 15
Baskin-Robbins to Follow Suit by January 1, 2008

CANTON, Mass. (August 27, 2007) -- Dunkin' Donuts today announced that all its menu offerings nationwide will be zero grams trans fat by October 15, 2007. This includes the brand's signature doughnuts. Doughnuts with zero grams trans fat are currently being served in Philadelphia and New York City. To date, the zero grams trans fat doughnuts have been served in approximately 400 restaurants throughout the country as part of a nationwide blind test over a period of four months.

In addition, Baskin-Robbins' offerings, including its ice cream inclusions and ribbons, will be zero grams trans fat by January 1, 2008.

capable of performing "magic" with a doomed project and making sure it succeeds. Project management is fast becoming a well-documented science with a comprehensive body of knowledge. It involves managing a project through knowledge, tools, and skills. In order to complete a project successfully, we use a project management process to achieve the final goal of delivering the desired quality within the allocated budget and timeline. The project management process focuses on resources and gets people committed and motivated to achieve the goals of the project.

The Project Management Body of Knowledge (PMBOK®) is a global standard from the Project Management Institute (PMI), and it defines project management as the application of knowledge, skills, and techniques to project activities in order to meet the stakeholder needs and expectations: "Project management is accomplished through the application and integration of various project management processes such as initiating, planning, executing, monitoring and controlling, and closing." The project manager is assigned during the initial stages and is the person primarily responsible for accomplishing the stated project objectives. Project managers often talk of a triple constraint—project scope, time, and cost—in managing competing project requirements. Project quality is affected by balancing these three factors.

Managing a project involves the following:

- Identifying all the requirements
- Establishing clear and achievable objectives
- Balancing the competing demands for quality, scope, time, and cost
- Adapting the specifications, plans, and expectations of the various stakeholders

Benefits of Project Management

A plethora of literature pertaining to project management refers to partially failed projects or projects that were complete failures. So the primary challenge of project management is to ensure that the stakeholder's investment in projects is fully maximized. Project management helps us to reduce problems through execution of project risk management principles. Lessons are learned and documented so that the same mistakes are not made the next time a similar project is undertaken. To summarize, benefits of project management include the following:

- Improving your chances of project success and delivering the expected benefits for the project
- Avoiding stress and increasing satisfaction for all stakeholders
- Completing projects within schedule, within budget, and with acceptable quality
- Optimizing use of organizational resources
- Enabling customer focus and introducing quality focus
- Reducing risks of unexpected events and project failure

PROJECT LIFE CYCLE AND PRODUCT LIFE CYCLE

There are life cycles for all kinds of activities associated with project management, but probably the two most important are the project life cycle and the product life cycle.

The project life cycle refers to a typical sequence of phases and sequential time progression of a project. The project life cycle can also be defined as "phases associated with a project." If we use the historic definition of a project as being "an idea," then we can suggest that a typical project life cycle goes through these phases: Conceive the idea, Develop the idea, Execute the idea, and finally Finish the idea (i.e., finish the project). Note the acronym CDEF is an easy way to remember the typical phases of the project life cycle.

The phases identify key aspects of a project, such as deliverables associated with each phase, people involved with each phase, and control and approval of each phase. This last point is important to note. As the project goes forward from one phase to another, it goes through a control gate, also called a stage gate. This is an executive control point for the project. You declare the overall status of the project as satisfactory after a complete analysis of the project goals, risks, budget, technology, and resources. If the results of the project at the stage gate are not satisfactory, you don't move forward and the project is stopped. The idea is to save any further loss of money on a doomed project.

Figure 1.2 Project Life Cycle Phases

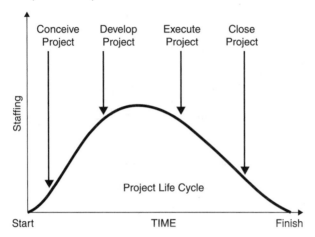

The project life cycle could be associated with a product life cycle. In which case, upon completing its typical sequence, the project life cycle produces a product. In some application domains, such as software development, the project life cycle parallels the product life cycle from start to finish. Note that the term widely used for a product life cycle for software development is systems development life cycle (SDLC). Most organizations consider the project life cycle to be part of the product life cycle and both are closely interrelated. However, in some application domains, such as manufacturing, the product life cycle may be larger than the project life cycle. Once a project life cycle designs and produces a product, the product life cycle continues with stages such as operations, distribution, and spinoff. While the first four phases map to the product life cycle satisfactorily,

Figure 1.3 Stage Gates: Control Points for Projects

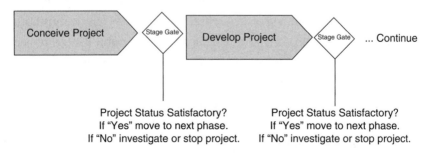

Figure 1.4 Comparison of Project and Product Life Cycles

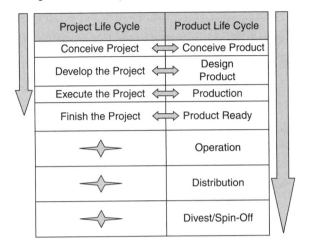

the last three phases of the product life cycle don't necessarily map to the project life cycle. This is graphically illustrated in the figure above.

WHAT IS THE ROLE AND RESPONSIBILITY OF A PROJECT MANAGER?

A project manager is assigned during the initiation phase of the project and is solely responsible for the success of the project. The project manager is anyone within the company who has the necessary knowledge and skills to perform the duties required by this role. Depending upon the scope of the project, the role can be either a full-time or a part-time responsibility. The project manager can be a senior manager or even a trained junior manager or employee. The project manager can be from systems analysis or from any business unit. The primary responsibility of the project manager is to ensure that the business objectives for the project are met.

The major responsibilities of the project manager include the following:

- Guide the project team to its goal to deliver a high quality project on time, within budget, and with no surprises

- Manage the planning, organizing, executing, controlling, and reporting of the project through all phases to ensure successful implementation

- Develop and coordinate resources
- Communicate across the organizational hierarchy and with stakeholders
- Motivate and nurture team members by providing feedback, coaching, and rewards
- Evaluate risks to senior management and manage those risks effectively throughout the project life cycle
- Solve problems—projects rarely progress as planned

A review of different job descriptions will reveal several unique competencies expected of a project manager. So even though it may appear that there is no standard job description for an expert project manager, on closer examination, a certain profile will emerge. We have summarized the profile of a typical project manager in Figure 1.5.

Figure 1.5 Project Manager Roles

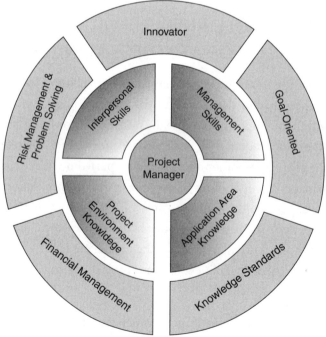

Some core competencies of a project manager are the following:

Project-Related Competencies

- Effectively applies methodology and enforces project standards
- Identifies resources needed and assigns individual responsibilities
- Creates and executes project work plans
- Manages day-to-day operational aspects of a project and its scope
- Reviews deliverables prepared by team before passing to client
- Prepares for engagement reviews and quality assurance procedures
- Minimizes exposure and risk on project
- Ensures project documents are complete, current, and stored appropriately
- Tracks and reports team hours and expenses on a weekly basis

Financial Management

- Understands basic revenue models, profit/loss statements, and cost-to-completion projections, and makes decisions accordingly
- Accurately forecasts revenue, profitability, margins, bill rates, and utilization
- Assures legal documents are completed and signed
- Manages budget and project accounting

Communication

- Facilitates team and client meetings effectively
- Holds regular status meetings with project team
- Keeps project team well informed of changes within the organization and of general corporate news
- Effectively communicates relevant project information to superiors
- Delivers engaging, informative, well-organized presentations
- Resolves and/or evaluates issues in a timely fashion
- Understands how to communicate difficult/sensitive information tactfully

The project manager should also be good at understanding the project environment since most projects are planned and implemented in a social, economic, and environmental context. The project manager should consider the project in its cultural, international, political, and physical environmental contexts.

While the focus of this book is not on general management or interpersonal skills, such skills are essential qualifications and a review of sample job descriptions suggests that most organizations require them. The project manager must have organizational and interpersonal skills such as:

- Effective communication with stakeholders
- Ability to influence and negotiate
- Leadership and motivation
- Conflict management
- Proactive risk management and problem solving

Does the Project Manager Need to Be Certified to Practice?

A popular certification is Project Management Professional (PMP) offered by the Project Management Institute, which has established a baseline to ensure standards upon which industry can rely. But you don't need to become certified to engage in project management. More information on certification is provided in the last chapter of this book.

OTHER ROLES ON THE PROJECT TEAM

Apart from the project manager, there are other key players on the project team. Let us briefly introduce some of them:

- Executive Steering Committee: Many large organizations have an executive steering committee which is composed of the president and his senior executives. Their responsibilities include approving projects for implementation, defining and communicating short- and long-term corporate goals, as well as giving guidance with respect to the availability of resources for projects.

- Project Sponsor: This is typically the department head of the business area requesting the new project, or a senior executive. The project sponsor defines the project, makes sure it fits within departmental and corporate goals, provides resources, kicks off the project at the initial meeting, and receives regular status reports. The project sponsor maintains contact with the project until its completion by establishing an effective working relationship with the project manager and removes any major barriers that will prevent project success.

- Functional Manager: The departmental managers or resource managers provide resources to the project manager. In a matrixed structure, the manager has full control over the resource but works closely with the project manager to make sure that the team member is meeting his or her project commitments. The functional manager is a stakeholder and plays a critical role on a project.

- Project Team Members: Team members are responsible for the overall execution of the project. In a matrixed team structure, a team member will represent the project interests of his or her respective departmental area within the corporation. However, the management of the team is the responsibility of the project manager.

- Business Architect or Analyst: The architect is charged with ensuring that the right set of requirements is documented and understood. A requirements document is typically a comprehensive description that focuses on the problems to be solved, not on the solution to those problems.

- Quality Team: Typically, a quality management unit will oversee the activities of the quality team. The team facilitates project development, conducts technical reviews at review points where appropriate, provides support and guidance to the development team throughout the project, and ensures projects conform to standards. The team also performs post-project reviews.

- Customer: This is the end user who benefits from the project deliverables. The customer defines the project and tests its results.

PROJECT MANAGEMENT PROCESS GROUPS

Project management activities can be categorized into process groups that represent project activity phases. Many organizations today have adopted the official standard for project management processes illustrated in figure 1.6 below. This specifies all the project management processes or activities that are used or required by the project team to manage any project in any industry. The constituent project management processes are initiating, planning, executing, monitoring and controlling, and closing. We will cover each of these process groups in detail in the next chapter. But we will define the process groups briefly below:

- Initiating: Introduces the project and the project manager and defines the charter for the project.

- Planning: Describes the project scope in more detail. Detailed project plans for schedule, cost, risk, quality, and communications amongst others are defined here. A realistic project baseline is committed to.

- Executing: The project has begun and the project manager uses various tools and techniques to make sure that the project is progressing smoothly.

- Monitoring and Controlling: The project manager monitors the project for deviations from cost, schedule, or quality and takes corrective action if needed.

- Closing: The focus of this process is on acceptance and approval of the project deliverables and documenting lessons learned.

Figure 1.6 Project Management Process Groups

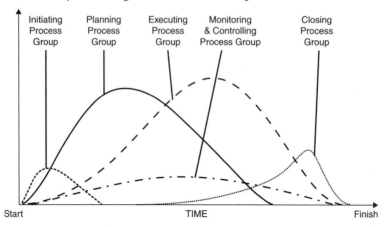

Knowledge Areas

In addition to the above five process groups, the Project Management Body of Knowledge introduces nine knowledge areas that interact with the project management process groups. The knowledge areas should be viewed as "knowledge requirements" for successful project management of each of the process groups introduced in figure 1.6. Some of the knowledge areas are introduced formally in the second half of this book, while the others are covered as part of the five process groups. The nine knowledge areas are the following:

1. Integration Management
2. Scope Management
3. Time Management
4. Cost Management
5. Quality Management
6. Human Resource Management
7. Communications Management
8. Risk Management
9. Procurement Management

Application Area Knowledge

Occasionally, we make reference to application areas. These areas are listed below with examples:

- Functional departments: Human resources, production, inventory, and marketing
- Technical disciplines: Information technology, software development, construction engineering, manufacturing engineering, and research & development
- Management specializations: new product development, supply chain management
- Industry groups: fabrication, chemical, automotive, farming

Application areas are unique because each has a set of accepted standards and practices, often codified in regulations, and each may use different methods and tools.

PORTFOLIO AND PROGRAM MANAGEMENT

This is an area of growing importance within the field of project management. A program is a group of related projects which are managed in a co-ordinated way so as to obtain benefits and control as well as gain efficiency on time, cost, and technology not available from managing them individually. Programs involve a series of related undertakings. The Olympics is a good example of a program. We could even consider the Winter Olympics and Summer Olympics as two program categories under the Olympic program. Each of these program categories has many projects, such as building a stadium or running an event like the Ice Hockey Tournament.

The Olympics is a cyclical recurring event: Should we regard the Olympics as a program or a project? The question we must immediately clarify here is: are we talking about an individual event or the Olympics as a whole?

- If we are talking about the entire Olympics, this is a program.
- If we are talking about an event, this is a project, as it is unique with a defined beginning and end.

A portfolio is a collection of projects or programs and other work that are grouped together to facilitate effective management to meet strategic business objectives. Figure 1.7 illustrates the relation between projects, programs, and the portfolio.

Figure 1.7 Portfolios, Programs, and Projects

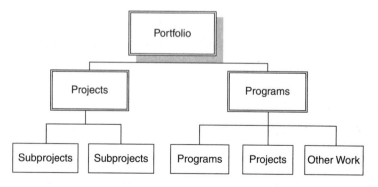

ROLE OF PROJECT MANAGEMENT OFFICE

A project management office (PMO) is an organizational unit used to centralize and coordinate the management of projects. A PMO oversees the management of projects, programs, or a combination of both. The projects supported or administered by the PMO need not be related other than that they are being managed together.

A project manager is responsible for delivering specific project objectives within the constraints of the project, while a PMO is an organizational structure with specific mandates that can include an enterprise-wide perspective. The project manager manages the scope, schedule, cost, and quality of the products of the work packages, while the PMO manages overall risk, opportunity, and the interdependencies among projects.

Projects have to be aligned with an organization's strategic plan. Projects are generally a means of organizing activities, which cannot be undertaken within an organization's normal operational schedule.

Important Questions

In this final section, we discus two important questions: what are the benefits of project management, and when must we practice formal project management?

Since formal project management might be time-consuming, when must one adopt formal project management practices? In our introduction we introduced various examples of a project, such as cooking a meal, planning a 50th wedding anniversary, or building a boat. Now that you have a foundation in project management, you might be wondering when you *must* adopt project management formally.

Cooking a unique vegan meal might typically involve five activities, such as locating a good recipe, identifying the ingredients, following the recipe instructions, completing the meal, and preparing it for serving on the dinner table. Even though this may be the first time you have ever cooked a vegan meal for a guest, you may not need to follow formal project management practice. So a key factor that will help you decide whether you must conduct formal project management practice is to ask yourself the following simple questions: Will this project require more than one person? Is the project likely to undergo significant changes? In either case, today's tools and automation make it feasible to use project management techniques on quite small projects. Further, formal project management techniques are invaluable when managing changes to a project. If it is an innovative or complex project, then you should probably adopt a formal project management methodology.

With innovation comes complexity. This requires implementation of several more activities to minimize uncertainty. Your best bet is to adopt formal project management practice. What are the risks of not following project management formally? The risks could be many; for examples, you might experience project delay, project failure, going over the allocated budget, or unhappy customers.

PROJECT MANAGEMENT IN ACTION

Kool Web Design is a Web design consulting company that was started by two classmates, Bob and Mary, upon graduation from an e-commerce program. When they first started, Bob focused on programming while Mary did Web design and training. They soon hired several part-time programmers to help them. Their business was successful and profitable in the first two years largely due to rewarding contracts from area businesses. But by the end of the third year of operation, Kool Web Design started experiencing critical problems. They were unable to:

- Deliver websites to their customers on schedule
- Provide quality Web applications—time and money were being spent on fixing defects
- Meet the needs of their best clients
- Control costs—business was not profitable in the third year

They were seeing issues such as:

- Communication problems

- A lot of "surprises" and issues that consumed their time
- Poorly estimated projects

Bob and Mary had both missed an opportunity to take a project management course at college. They recalled that their friend, Sam, who had taken a couple of project management elective courses while at college, was excited about the discipline of project management. Upon graduation he had intentionally selected a job with a consulting company that was strong on project management.

So one fine day, Bob invited his friend, Sam, over to Kool Web Design for a lunch meeting to hear what he had to say about the problems he and Mary were facing. He described how his small business operated and implemented projects. He listed the problems they were facing and asked if it was simply growing pains or lack of expertise in project management that led to the crisis.

Sam quickly noted that Kool Web Design, while being innovative, completed projects without a road map or a project plan and lacked a disciplined project management approach. They had no project management methodology, did not use any project software for scheduling and reporting, and had almost no tools to help them with project management. Finally, they had no project communication processes in place and were inexperienced in the areas of cost estimation and project risk management.

Bob asked Sam if he would consider joining them as a partner to help them introduce project management processes and tide them over the current crisis. Sam was looking to enhance his career in project management, so he gladly offered to join them as a project manager.

Sam had excellent communication skills, he was detail oriented, and had very good interpersonal skills. Within three months of joining, he introduced a formal project management framework. He trained Bob, Mary, and the several contract employees on the basics of project management and how to get the right work done well. He purchased several licenses for an off-the-shelf project management software tool and showed them how to use the software. He created several standard templates to help them manage their projects. The templates sped up the production of documents such as project charters, scope and requirements document, activities, estimates, and the project plan.

The following key activities and processes were introduced at the company:

- Identifying the customer problem clearly and producing a scope statement that was signed off by stakeholders
- Identifying business requirements early on and converting them into project specifications. A prototype was created where possible so that the specifications could be validated by the customers.
- Estimating effort and costs using at least two techniques
- Identifying, quantifying, and mitigating risks and controlling them throughout the project at weekly meetings
- Creating a live project plan that acted as a road map for the entire project
- Introducing project quality management processes
- Facilitating communication and collaboration throughout the project
- Monitoring and controlling project cost and schedule for variances. Sam had introduced earned value which allowed them to track schedules and costs.
- Keeping track of metrics and lessons learned and using them for project planning on their next Web project

Within 12 months Sam had turned things around. The company was able to deliver professional websites and quality management processes worked well. Formal reviews and quality control reduced the bugs in the websites. There was less rework and this single aspect helped the business tremendously. Projects were estimated much better and cost budgeting and control processes were working well. "Surprises" and issues were reduced drastically due to proactive risk analysis and risk response planning. Communication problems with stakeholders were dramatically reduced due to frequent exchange of documents, reviews, and meetings. There was substantial stakeholder satisfaction and, once again, opportunities for repeat business from their best customers.

TEST YOURSELF

1. Which of the following are projects?

    a) Cooking a meal or running a restaurant?
    b) Building a boat or operating a marina?
    c) Upgrading your OS or playing a video game?

    Answer for a) While cooking a unique vegan meal for the first time can be a project, regularly cooking lunch or dinner in a restaurant might not be a project.

2. On your own, list three examples of projects and three more examples that are not projects.

3. What are the benefits of using project management?

4. List five key skills that a project manager must have.

KEY POINTS TO REMEMBER

- Projects are temporary and have definite beginning and ending dates. Projects exist to bring about a unique product, service, or result. A project must achieve its goal within a specific time frame and budget and must meet the quality expectations of the funding entity.

- Projects are considered complete only when the deliverables of the project meet the expectations of the stakeholders.

- Projects may be organized into programs or portfolios and may be managed centrally by a project management office.

- Project management is both an art and a science. It is a discipline that uses a set of tools and techniques to define, plan, organize, and monitor the work of project activities. *Project managers* are responsible for leading a team to carry out activities successfully.

- Difference between projects and operations: Projects produce unique products, services, or results, whereas operations are ongoing and use repetitive processes that mostly produce the same result.

- Skills every project manager should possess: Communication, budgeting, organizational, problem solving, negotiation and influencing, leading, and team building.

Project Management: A Case Study

INTRODUCTION

In this chapter, we expand the five project management process groups introduced in the previous chapter using a complete case study as a foundation. It will help you get your first project under way easily using formal project management processes.

WHAT'S AHEAD	

• Project management: learning by example
• Project management process groups
• Project management case study
	• Examples of:
	  • Initation
	  • Planning
	  • Execution
	  • Monitoring and Control
	  • Closing

IN THE REAL WORLD

Projects are complex and they need to be managed in an integrative manner by the project manager. The Vista case study that follows integrates the five stages of project management and helps you understand the key project management processes that a project manager will use for a typical project. The project manager applies the five process groups—project initiating, project planning, project executing, project monitoring and controlling, and project closing to ensure project success.

Case Study Background

Anita Rains works for Boston Universal Group (BUG) as a project manager. The company is a leader in Microsoft Office applications consulting. They are known nationally for providing consulting, training, and services involving Microsoft systems, especially in the Office suite. They have about 200 employees, 50 laptops, and 160 workstations at the work center.

With the introduction of the Windows Vista operating system there is pressure from their customers to support the Vista platform. Boston Universal Group has subsequently decided to upgrade the operating system on their workstations from XP to Vista. Anita has been asked to champion this initiative. She has worked in the organization for over a decade and recalls the chaos during the upgrade to Windows XP from Windows 98. As a trained professional in project management, she decides to use the best practices as defined in the Project Management Body of Knowledge (PMBOK).

KEY CONCEPTS

The Project Management Institute (PMI) defines a framework for project management, which allows project managers to apply accepted practices and procedures to manage projects. The structure of the PMBOK guide includes Project Phases, Project Life Cycles, Process Groups, and Knowledge

Areas. There are five project process groups: initiating, planning, executing, controlling and monitoring, and closing. Project managers will use this framework only as a model. They will interpret the aforementioned guide in a variety of ways. Depending upon the nature and size of the project, not all processes might be used.

This raises the issue of what is considered a small project, medium project, or large project. A project can be considered small if it has a total duration of less than 3 months, medium if it is between 3 and 12 months in duration, and large if it is more than a year in duration. Dollar amounts may also decide the size—if the amount is less than $100,000, then it is likely a small project. If the budget is between $100,000 and $1,000,000, it can be regarded as a medium project, and anything larger is a large project. Large projects require a lot of detail and generate a lot of documentation, both internal and external.

PROJECT INITIATION

During the initiating process group, the start of a new project is authorized. Some organizations use a business case as a trigger for the project initiation phase. Also, a statement of work (SOW) can trigger the initiation phase. The main goal of this phase is to formally select and start off projects. This process group recognizes that the organization is committed to starting the project.

Key outputs include the following:

- Assigning the project manager
- Identifying key stakeholders
- Establishing a project charter
- Establishing a preliminary project scope statement

Getting the signatures on the charter from senior management and stakeholders will ensure a sound foundation for the project. This document sets the stage for the subsequent development work. See an example of the project charter, as created by management, in table 2.1.

Figure 2.1 Initiating the Project

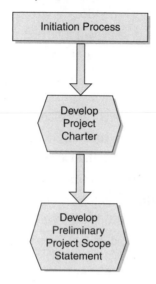

PROJECT PLANNING

Once the project has been initiated, the project manager plans the project. The planning process refines the project goals and documents the best way to achieve them. Here you would describe the project scope in more detail and come up with project plans for schedule, cost, risk, quality, and communications amongst others. A realistic project baseline is approved by all stakeholders and the project manager secures formal approval to proceed to the next phase.

Planning is the most creative part of the project for the project manager. A variety of project plans are produced—the most common ones are project timeline, risk plan, cost and budget, quality plan, and communications plan.

The Vista Project can be considered to be a medium project due to the allocated budget of $150,000 and therefore almost all the planning processes will be used by Anita Rains. Note that procurement processes pertain to timely purchase of Vista Business Edition licenses.

Anita decides to focus on the following key documents for the planning phase of the project:

• Project scope statement

Table 2.1 Project Charter

Project Charter

Project Title: Upgrade to Windows Vista
Project Start Date: Feb 2009
Project Finish Date: May 2009

Budget Information: BUG has allocated a budget of $150,000 to upgrade the computers from XP to Vista Business Edition. The major costs will be labor and licenses for Vista Business Edition. Additional contingency costs for hardware will be set aside as well.

This project is critical for the future competitiveness of the corporation. The project will be completed with the highest standards. The data integrity and privacy of all users will be protected during this migration.

Stakeholders:
➤ The organization as a whole (all desktop users)
➤ Management, IT operations dept, developers, quality team

Anita Rains is assigned as the project manager.
As the project's stakeholders your signature below indicates that you support the initiative as well as the schedule and budget.

(*Space for every key party to sign the charter to demonstrate their commitment to the project.*)

Print Name: *Signature:*

Date: *Title:*

- Project work breakdown structure
- Milestone Report
- Project Closure Report

Once the project charter has been signed, the next thing to do is to develop the project scope statement. If the project scope statement is well written, it will minimize confusion about the project boundaries and will also communicate clearly to the stakeholders the work associated with the project. The scope document should have the following characteristics: a clear goal with information about the expected duration of the project, its justification, description of all objectives, project requirements—broken down into features where possible—known issues, risks and obstacles, and a description of deliverables with brief performance or completion criteria.

In table 2.2 we have created a sample project scope statement for the Vista Project. A good scope statement typically describes the following aspects of a project:

- Project description
- The justification: problem or opportunity
- Goals and objectives
- Deliverables
- Milestones
- Assumptions
- Limits and constraints
- The statement of work
- The customer interface

Not all projects will require all sections, but the project manager should check to see that all sections have been thought through.

Figure 2.2 describes the planning processes. It begins with planning and developing the project scope and continues with the project plan. The planning process group is the heart and soul of project management and has the largest number of processes, all of which contribute toward producing a useful and robust project plan. Several chapters in this book are dedicated to this topic. The project plan answers questions such as:

- What work must be done?
- What deliverable will this work produce?
- Who will do the work?

Table 2.2 Project Scope Statement

Project Title: Upgrade to Windows Vista
Project Start Date: Feb 10, 2009
Project Finish Date: May 21, 2009

Project Goal: Upgrade 160 workstations running Windows XP to Windows Vista operating system (OS) within the time frame of four months.

Description of All Objectives, Characteristics, or Requirements:
- Determine software conflicts.
- Steps for upgrading to Windows Vista:

  Step 1: Assess hardware requirements
  Step 2: Back up important data
  Step 3: Upgrade to Windows Vista

- Determine requirements for installing Windows Vista.
- Upgrade all PCs with additional hardware and memory.
- Migrating to Windows Vista: migrate user settings; migrate the entire OS.
- Investigate applications that do not migrate successfully and upgrade them.
- Do complete quality test.
- Provide training to users for the new OS.

Project Justification: The business reasons (problem or opportunity): Boston Universal Group (BUG) focuses on Microsoft customers and most of their customer base has upgraded to the Vista operating system. Doing the same at BUG will give the consultants an additional level of comfort when dealing with the latest Office products and operating system. Also, recently BUG has received a major contract to create training content based on Vista.

(continued)

Table 2.2 *(continued)*

Known Issues, Risks, Obstacles:
- Several applications are known to be incompatible with the new OS.
- We should inform the users of such incompatibility and resolve issues.
- There are some reports of security issues with Vista. IT will patch the new OS immediately upon installation.
- Some laptops are out in the field with sales people.

Assumptions:
Funding is available for migration and IT resources are available as scheduled. Users will surrender their desktops and laptops as scheduled for migration.
Summary of deliverables:
- Successful migration to new Vista OS
- Successfully trained users on the new operating system

Project Success Criteria:
The goal is to complete the project within four months and within the allocated budget. The users will receive a survey six months after migration to determine if the new OS is satisfactory and meets their business needs.

- When will it be done?
- What criteria will be used to ensure quality?
- What can go wrong?

Upon completion of the project scope statement, the project team develops a work breakdown structure (WBS) for the project. This is a deliverable-oriented tool breaking the project scope into smaller packages. Table 2.3 shows a sample WBS for the Vista Project.

Figure 2.2 Planning the Project

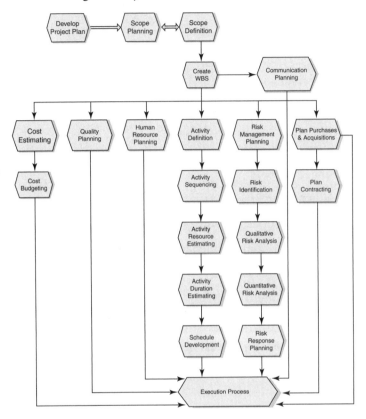

Typically, the above information is entered into a project management tool like Microsoft Project to generate a network and critical path for the project. The Gantt chart that is developed from this is used as a baseline for monitoring and controlling the project.

Risks

With the help of the team, Anita developed a list of technical risks for the Vista Project and generated a risk response plan:

1. Hardware and hard disk space requirements may increase the cost

    • Risk response: Keep management informed

Table 2.3 Sample WBS for the Vista Project

Project Tasks

1. Initiation
   a. Project kickoff
   b. Gain senior management approval
   c. Determine major stakeholders

2. Planning
   a. Gather the upgrade details from Microsoft and other sources
   b. List applications running on a PC
   c. Check H/W compatibility and space requirements
   d. Mock run on a test PC
   e. Test Vista compatibility
   f. Upgrade running S/W, if required
   g. Rollback plan for critical machines

3. Execution
   a. Procure of OS license keys
   b. Order the H/W upgrades
   c. Gather of resources
   d. Install the H/W and the OS
   e. Create Training/help desk
   f. Steps for upgrading to Windows Vista
      i. Assess hardware requirements
      ii. Back up important data
      iii. Upgrade to Windows Vista
      iv. Migrate user settings

(continued)

Table 2.3 *(continued)*

4. Control and Monitoring

    a. Keeping the project on schedule

    b. Keeping the cost on budget

    c. Monitoring the impact on users

    d. Resolving issues/concerns

5. Closing

    a. Conduct project closure

    b. Document lessons learned

    c. Archive the project documents to the company repository

---

2. Incompatible software may delay the upgrade

- Risk response: Do rigorous testing on a prototype up front

3. Recovery plans

- Risk response: Create a rollback plan for critical machines
- Create a backup of all data

4. Vista security concerns

- Risk response: Perform adequate testing
- Involve the development department

5. Impact on daily productivity of workforce

- Risk response: Perform the upgrade only during the evenings

Anita was able to identify several nontechnical risks as well from her previous experience on a Windows 98 to XP migration project. The key risks are listed below:

- Getting resources on schedule as promised
- Users do not turn in the desktop for migration as scheduled

- Users on vacation or on business travel are not able to turn in laptops
- Communication risks: users misunderstand technical issues

PROJECT EXECUTION

The project has begun and the project manager uses various processes and tools to make sure that the project is progressing smoothly. During this phase, the project manager obtains reports in a timely manner and ensures that the project's requirements and objectives, as specified in the scope statement, are being met. The project manager also motivates the project team so that its efforts are focused on the project deliverables.

During this phase of the project, Anita works closely with the project team and coordinates other resources to carry out the project plan. She also organizes project team meetings to gather additional information. If any new risks come up, Anita mitigates them and also communicates them to the stakeholders. She reviews milestone reports and other variance reports generated by the project scheduling software. A typical milestone report is illustrated below.

Table 2.4 Milestone Report

Milestone	Date	Resource	Status
Initiation phase	Feb 15	Anita	Completed
Planning: Gathering the upgrade details	Feb 28	Jen	Completed
Planning: Applications running on a PC	Mar 2	Mary	In progress
Planning: Check H/W compatibility	Mar 15	Das	Not started

The key processes associated with project execution are illustrated in figure 2.3. The goal of the project processes here is to create the deliverables or service that the customer wants. The planned resources are put into play, and the quality team ensures quality by executing the test system. Information distribution to stakeholders is a key responsibility

Figure 2.3 Executing the Project

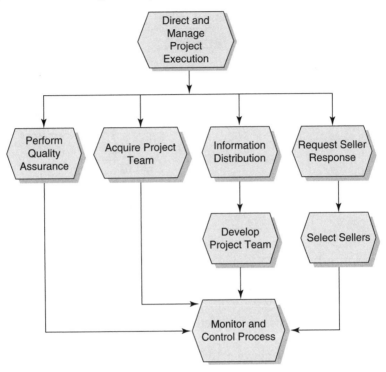

of the project manager. If the project involves outsourcing, requesting seller responses and selecting sellers is coordinated by the project manager.

MONITORING AND CONTROL

During this phase of the project, the project manager monitors cost, quality, and schedule. The project performance is monitored by tracking the baseline schedule for variances from the project management plan. We ensure that project objectives are met by monitoring and measuring progress and taking corrective action when necessary. The following key activities occur during this phase:

- Decision to accept inspected deliverables
- Recommending corrective actions such as rework of deliverables

Figure 2.4 Monitoring and Controlling the Project

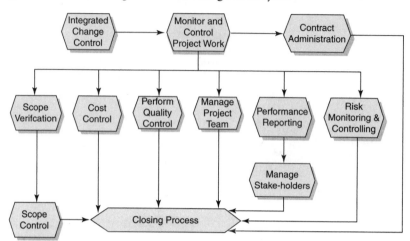

- Updates to project plan, schedule, and budget
- Evaluation checklists are completed

In addition to the above activities, during this phase of the project, Anita tracks change-control requests and updates the project plan. If there is change in project scope, she generates new forecasts and communicates this to the project team and stakeholders. Due to increase in scope, there may be more work to be done, but the original deadline might still be firm. Anita will have to compress the schedule using techniques such as fast-tracking or crashing the schedule. Figure 2.4 communicates key processes that are controlled; they include cost, quality, project team, risk, contracts, and stakeholders.

PROJECT CLOSING

The focus of this process is on formal acceptance and approval of the project deliverables by the sponsors and on documenting lessons learned. This phase focuses on administrative closure; if a contractor was used, then the quality of the services is evaluated and the contracted amount is paid in a timely manner. It is important to hold a customer acceptance meeting and conduct a deliverables review. The project manager also sets up a meeting to document lessons learned from the project.

Such information will come in handy should the organization become involved in another project of this nature. If project scheduling tools are used, you already have a repository of the WBS and risks documented in the project plan. You can save this as a template for future use.

Note that the project manager also uses this opportunity to provide feedback on individual performance. If there are individual performance issues pertaining to any team member, the project manager must comment on the poor performance in private. Possible attributes for discussion could be timeliness, quality of deliverables, and participation in the team. If there are reasons beyond the control of the team member, they should be investigated as well. Frequently, the problems are due to the project manager not providing timely training to the team.

A final project report is also created and published. The content of such a report is indicated in the table below.

Table 2.5 Project Closure Report

Client Name
Project Background and Description
Summary of Project Results
Reason for Closing the Project
Deliverables
Project Schedule: Original and Actual Start and End Dates
Project Team
Outstanding Risks
Budget and Financial Information: Original and Actual
Action Plan
Ongoing Support
Next Steps or Transition Plan
Project Closure Approval

(continued)

Table 2.5 (*continued*)

Appendix A
Project Management–Related Documentation

Appendix B
Product-Related Documentation

PROJECT MANAGEMENT IN ACTION

Project Vista is a good example of project management in action. We saw an example of how Boston Universal Group applied the project management framework to a project. Anita and her team successfully finished the project using the five process groups—initiating, planning, executing, monitoring and control, and closing. Here is a summary of what happened.

During the initiation process, the organization created a charter which was signed by all key stakeholders within the organization. Anita was assigned the role of project manager during this phase of the project.

During the planning phase, Anita created a comprehensive scope statement, work breakdown structure, network flowchart, and project schedule. She used Microsoft Project to generate visual reports like a Gantt chart, network flowchart, and an activity calendar for communicating with the project team and stakeholders. The project software also generated a critical path which Anita used to monitor and track the project. Finally, a comprehensive and formal project plan document was created. This document was used to guide the project through the key stages of project execution and control.

The execution processes ensure that the project is progressing smoothly. During this phase, Anita obtained reports in a timely manner and made sure that the project's requirements and objectives, as specified in the scope statement, were being met. Anita worked closely with the project team and coordinated all resources to carry out the project plan. She organized effective weekly team meetings to gather additional information from the project team. The risk management plan was always on the agenda, and the following questions were constantly asked: Has any risk materialized? Has the ranking of any existing risk changed? Are there any new risks?

During the monitoring and control phase of the project, Anita tightly managed cost, quality, and schedule variances and used her communication skills to ensure that stakeholders were informed of project progress and completion of key milestones. As with many projects, she had scope changes to deal with. However, she managed such scope changes using a change control procedure originally approved during the planning stage. She used her negotiation techniques to ensure that the scope changes accompanied a realistic revised schedule.

Finally, Project Vista went through the project closing processes. This involved activities such as customer acceptance, meeting with the project sponsor, project review with the project team, and a project closure report. Anita updated the project plan and project metrics after this meeting. When a similar project is implemented again in the future, she will use this project as a template for effort and cost estimation as well as project planning.

TEST YOURSELF

1. Consider the five project management process groups—initiating, planning, executing, monitoring and control, and closing. During which phase of the project will the project manager spend the most amount of time and the least amount of time? Explain.

2. For each of the items listed in the project management plan for the Vista Project, can you provide summary comments on the role of the project manager? What skills will the project manager be using at each stage? What tools and techniques will the project manager use? Make assumptions using the Vista Project example as a reference. Assume that the charter has been created already.

KEY POINTS TO REMEMBER

Project Process Groups

Every project will use these five project management process groups:

- Initiating
- Planning
- Execution
- Monitoring and controlling
- Closing

Authorization for the Next Phase

You must obtain a "go/no go" decision from the sponsors before the project moves on to the next major phase. For example, at the end of the initiation phase, a "go/no go" decision can be made to apply further organizational resources. If the answer is no, the project is revised or killed.

Initiation Process

This phase identifies high-level business objectives and requirements and secures commitment to proceed by appointing a project manager who is authorized to apply resources to project activities. Specific objectives are to develop the high-level business goals and create a project charter.

Planning Process

This is the most creative and important step for the project manager, as it involves planning and organizing the project activities. Sample activities that occur during this stage are the following:

- Create a scope statement
- Create a work breakdown structure (WBS)

- Define and sequence project activities
- Estimate durations for activities; apply resources to the activities and determine costs for the project
- Develop a project schedule
- Create a budget and spending plan
- Create a formal quality plan
- Create a formal project communications plan
- Identify risks and plan to respond

Execution Process

The project has begun and the project manager uses various tools and techniques to make sure that the project progresses smoothly. During this phase of the project, the project manager does the following:

- Obtains reports in a timely manner
- Ensures that the project's requirements and objectives are being met
- Ensures that the team is guided, motivated, and kept on track

Monitoring and Control Process

As the project is being executed, it needs to be monitored and controlled. The key role of the project manager at this phase is to identify variances from the plan and take action. The project manager also undertakes the following activities:

- Manage change
- Monitor the milestone reports and other progress reports
- Monitor and control risks
- Monitor and control schedule and cost variance
- Make decisions on quality control issues such as corrective actions or rework of deliverables

Closing Process

Project closure is an important phase, as it is difficult sometimes to close a project. A project is closed when it is formally accepted by the sponsors. The key deliverables of this phase are the following:

- Document lessons learned
- Provide feedback to team members
- Complete project closure report
- Get sign-off from stakeholders
- Archive plans and resources for future use

Project Initiation: The Scope

INTRODUCTION

Every project needs well-defined, achievable goals and a road map for achieving them. The scope does this by defining all of the products, services, and results to be provided in the execution of the project. The scope statement is the single most important document in the project.

The scope must be complete and precise. If an architect forgets to include a garage in the plan for your new house, you will be really annoyed. In this case, the scope is incomplete. The scope must also be precise. If the architect only specifies two bathrooms, you are entitled to ask if they include baths and/or showers? In this case, the scope is imprecise.

The scope defines the expectations of all stakeholders and in particular, those of the customer. Mistakes and omissions in the scope document are the most frequent types of project management errors and also the most expensive to fix.

WHAT'S AHEAD

- There's no project without a charter
- What is the scope?
- Why is the scope so important?
- How do you create the scope?

- What are deliverables?
- The statement of work
- The triple constraint
- Errors in the scope are expensive

IN THE REAL WORLD

Suppose you decide to build a new house. Four questions immediately come to mind: What? How? When? Who?

1. What?

   A three bedroom house, with one and a half baths and a garage.

   These are the customer's requirements. We will refer to the document that defines these requirements as the specification, or spec. The scope also contains all of the technical requirements that must be met. For a house, these include all the zoning restrictions, electrical and plumbing codes, environmental regulations, etc.

2. How?

   A New England cape with brick walls, aluminum studs, a gabled roof, etc.

   This is the architect's plan, and it carefully defines all of the construction in great detail. We will refer to this as the design document. There is an important difference between the requirements and the design. The requirements describe the customer's needs and desires. In the case of the house, this is the *what* (three bedrooms). The design specifies *how* (brick walls, aluminum studs, etc). What may seem confusing is that the scope can contain both the requirements and the design.

3. When?

    We want to move in on December 1st.

    This is the schedule. It specifies all of the dates for the major deliverables, especially the end date for the project to be complete. It also specifies all of the intermediate milestones that must be achieved to get to the end result on time.

4. Who?

    Who does what? This is the statement of work (SOW). The SOW specifies the products and services to be supplied during the project.

KEY CONCEPTS

THE PROJECT CHARTER

A project does not exist until the charter is officially authorized. Only when the charter is approved can the project begin.

If you are assigned the position of project manager, the first question to ask is, "Can I see a copy of the charter?" If there is no charter, there is no project.

The charter contains a high-level description of the project and its objectives and maybe an overview of the business case, as well as any important constraints and assumptions. The most important aspect of the charter is that it grants to the project manager the authority to spend money and use the organization's resources to do the project.

Usually, everyone with an interest in the project signs the charter: clients, sponsors, senior managers, as well as the project manager. Doing so indicates their commitment to the success of the project. The signing of the charter is often a ceremonial event.

A project charter is not used to manage changes to the project. If large-scale project changes make the charter obsolete or outdated, a new charter should be issued. If a project manager feels the urge to update the charter, this is a sign that the current project is obsolete—a new project is probably required.

THE SCOPE

The scope statement is a document that completely and precisely specifies the sum of all the products, services, and results to be delivered as a project. This sets the right tone in that it recognizes the concept of the project as a deliverable. A project proceeds much better when the manager focuses on deliverables. Whether it is a document or a piece of hardware, you can recognize a deliverable. A half-done deliverable is of no use to anyone.

What is the final deliverable for the project? If we can recognize it, we will know when we are done. But to get there requires a lot of work and before the work starts, a lot of detailed planning. Some people want to rush in and start making something, but it is almost always a mistake. Planning comes first.

Once the charter exists, the project manager can start work and to the project manager, the first and most important step is the creation of the scope.

There are many important reasons for focusing on the scope. First, it is well established in project management literature that the most frequent cause of project failure is a poor scope document. Second, the scope defines what is to be delivered—and *only* what is to be delivered.

The statement of work (SOW) is the basis of the contract between the customer and the organization performing the project work. The length and complexity of the SOW depends on the size of the project and also the stage of the project. There may be several versions of the SOW over time. For example, there is often a preliminary SOW for a proposal phase. The winning bidder may then develop a more detailed SOW based on the particulars of their design for the project.

Whatever the stage of the project and whatever its size, the SOW contains the following types of information:

- Activities to be performed
- Deliverables resulting from those activities
- Review schedule and reporting criteria

Finally, there is a contract. There is some overlap between the contract and the other documents. A contract might include the scope and the design document by reference (e.g., the contract might say, "Build a house according to the attached documents"). The contract usually specifies the schedule at a high level, leaving the details to the project manager. All of the technical regulations that apply will also be referenced in the contract.

REQUIREMENTS VERSUS DESIGN

When creating the scope, the first thing to emphasize is the distinction between requirements and design. The scope may contain both what is required and how to build it. It is sometimes hard to distinguish the what from the how.

It is naive to think that one can completely specify what is to be done without some notion of how. Suppose you ask a builder to construct a house. You will give the builder a budget. However, the cost of the house will depend on the construction materials and the quality of the work, as well as the proposed design. While one can specify the requirements for the house (four bedrooms, two bathrooms, etc.), the cost will certainly depend on how it is built. Knowing the cost, one might change the requirements (three bedrooms, one and a half bathrooms).

Requirements cannot be specified without a context. Most projects have a requirements definition phase, and part of that phase includes preliminary design. The goal of this preliminary design work is not to prescribe how to do the job, but to demonstrate the project's feasibility.

Feasibility covers a multitude of issues. A preliminary design might demonstrate that performance requirements are achievable (e.g., that a software project's response time of less than one second is achievable or that the span of a bridge is buildable); that the cost is appropriate (enough design to conduct a parametric cost analysis); and that the schedule is achievable (a preliminary network diagram). It is necessary during the requirements definition phase to produce a realistic scope.

One of the keys to a clear scope is to distinguish between "shall" and "should." Use of "shall" means that the requirement must be satisfied. For example, compare the following:

- The device shall be waterproof.
- The device should be waterproof.

The first statement is a specific requirement, and the customer will expect that a test of "waterproof" will be conducted at delivery. One can envision all sorts of "waterproof" tests: take the device in the shower, drop it in a swimming pool, or even drop it in the ocean. Few devices can stand up to seawater. Using "should" says that waterproofing is merely a goal. The use of "should" is more ambiguous and can lead to disputes over what is meant.

ELEMENTS OF THE SCOPE

An important aspect of scope definition is to specify and control what is and is not included in the scope, and therefore, the project. The scope usually has less detail in the beginning of the project and more detail as project characteristics are refined. This means that the scope evolves over time, and a crucial part of project management is managing these changes. Customers, users, and even project staff often try to add requirements to the scope, additions which they think may be simply "nice to have." The project manager must guard against this and stick to the scope definition agreed to in the beginning of the project. In other words, the project manager must focus on refining the scope, not embellishing it.

The scope document is referred to when making all project decisions. Therefore, it should clearly outline project boundaries, making it easier for the project manager and team members to identify any and all work that must be completed. The scope typically describes the following aspects of a project:

- Project description
- The justification or opportunity
- Goals and objectives
- Deliverables
- Milestones
- Assumptions
- Limits and constraints
- The statement of work
- The customer interface

Project Description

This is the heart of the scope because the project requirements are laid out here. The product or service description explains the characteristics of the project and clearly defines the end goal. Project description clarity ensures that all stakeholders have a common understanding of the end product or service.

For each customer requirement, it helps to ask, "How will this requirement be tested?" If this cannot be answered, then the requirement description is probably too vague. Or if the resulting test is very complicated, perhaps the requirement is over-specified and some simplification is in order.

The Justification or Opportunity

The project's justification describes the business need, which is identified when the project is selected and authorized. A project's justification provides a benchmark for evaluating the trade-offs that arise during the project implementation.

For example, if an organization is losing business because a technological advance has outdated its internal network, a project may be authorized to upgrade the network. Suppose the new network upgrade requires a 50 percent increase in operational efficiencies. During the project, the goal of a 50 percent increase should be continually measured against the costs associated with upgrading. Trade-offs can be conducted to determine if a lower increase in speed (perhaps 45 percent) can be achieved at an earlier delivery date, or if the requirements can be met with a less expensive network. The project manager should constantly measure the current efficiency levels and compare them to the efficiency improvements defined in the scope.

It is important to continue to monitor the project's business need and its justification. Otherwise, a project may become obsolete before it is finished.

Goals and Objectives

The project's goals and objectives define the criteria that must be met to complete the project successfully. Every project must have objectives that are clear to all stakeholders. If the objectives are not clear, then different individuals may have different interpretations of the goals.

A useful guideline for assessing objectives is to ensure that they are all Specific, Measurable, Assignable, Realistic, and Time-related (SMART). Project objectives must also be consistent with the parent organization's mission, as well as policies and procedures.

Deliverables

The term deliverable is used frequently in project management because it focuses on outputs. Focusing on outputs helps define the boundaries of the project and keeps the team focused on the project goal.

A deliverable is a tangible product, result, or capability of the project and is usually subject to approval by the customer. The key word here is tangible. There should be nothing ambiguous about any of the deliverables, and it should be very clear when they are complete. The progress of the project can only be accurately assessed by measuring the completion of deliverables against the plan. Deliverables are therefore a fundamental component of the scope.

There are both intermediate and end deliverables. The end deliverable is the final product. A detailed and complete scope document might be an intermediate deliverable. For example, a document that identifies the user interface for a new software program is an intermediate deliverable, while the actual software program is the end deliverable.

To show how the work of the project will be completed, all deliverables should be defined in terms of tangible, verifiable products or services. Tangible deliverables are physical, specific products—you know them when you see them. They must also be verifiable in the sense that you must be able to tell if they are complete and up to standard. Detailed end-deliverable descriptions identify the necessary features for the product, provide a basis for the definition of the cost, schedule, and materials, and clarify the goals.

Milestones

A milestone is a significant event in the life of a project. The most important milestone, of course, is the completion date for the entire project. This is a schedule milestone, an event that has zero duration. Other milestones are intermediate and represent significant events. Typical milestones include completion dates for deliverables, acceptance dates for certifications and tests, and customer reviews and meeting dates.

Assumptions

Assumptions are the factors that are considered to be true. For example, the builder of a house may propose a schedule that assumes a building permit can be obtained in 30 days. This is stated without proof or demonstration. All assumptions must be clearly stated and monitored throughout the project. Assumptions often involve some risk, as in the above case where it was assumed that a permit can be obtained in 30 days.

Project managers must understand how the listed assumptions affect the project. Project assumptions may include technical conditions, schedule issues, or external events. An example of a technical assumption is a customer requirement to use a specific piece of hardware or machinery. The project manager would then need to define any related assumptions, such as the ability of the device to process the required number of transactions, the delivery date, etc. Schedule assumptions may include the delivery dates of hardware or software. Cost or funding assumptions may include borrowing constraints or the availability of capital.

Limits and Constraints

A constraint is a factor that limits the options for the project. Constraints may include performance requirements, such as meeting environmental regulations or recycling goals. Constraints may also include contractual provisions, budget and schedule limitations, as well as legal, accounting, and human resource provisions. Technical constraints are typically decided or negotiated during the development of the scope, while contractual provisions would usually be included in the SOW.

There are many types of constraints: a schedule constraint might be the imposition of a completion date; a resource constraint might be the availability of certain key personnel or equipment; a budget constraint might result from the availability of funds. Many constraints are found in industry standards, such as building codes, environmental regulations, and American National Standards Institute (ANSI) standards. These constraints will typically not be included in the scope, but are incorporated by reference. This means that the applicable document is referenced in the scope, and all of its conditions apply to the project.

When faced with a time or cost constraint, a trade-off analysis may be conducted to determine a workable solution (e.g., hiring outside expert consultants may accelerate the schedule but add cost). A trade-off typically affects many aspects of the project, so it is important to critically examine the assumptions involved and to determine which choices will have the most positive impact and least undesirable side effects.

The Statement of Work

The statement of work (SOW) defines who will do what and when, so the SOW is a statement of all products and services to be supplied. The content of the scope and SOW can overlap. Usually, the scope specifies what is to be performed, while the SOW specifies the tasks to be performed. For example, the SOW might say, "Build a house according to the attached scope." The SOW usually defines the overall schedule, and it is the basis for the legal contract.

The Customer Interface

The customer must sign off on the scope. This ensures that the customer has agreed to what is to be provided. Also, either the scope or the SOW should define the interface with the customer, in terms of reviews, regular progress reports, and acceptance criteria.

We see that the scope consists of the requirements (what), the design (how), the SOW (who and when), and the legal contract. Together these documents define the project and how it will be completed. The scope also includes the business case and company strategy, constraints and assumptions, acceptance criteria and approval requirements (how will we know when we are done?), risks, schedules, cost estimates and funding limitations, and change control requirements. Finally, of particular importance is the customer interface and review schedule (monthly review meetings with the customer). While the above information may be distributed in different ways throughout the various documents, it is essential that it all be completed and included somewhere. The above list is therefore a checklist for the information to be included in the scope.

THE TRIPLE CONSTRAINT

The triple constraint is a framework for understanding, managing, and balancing the competing demands of a project. Every project is affected by the triple constraint of scope, cost, and time (or schedule). You cannot change any one of these parameters without impacting the other two. Quality, which is defined as "conformance to requirements" is firmly placed at the center of the triangle, and this is best understood by considering that product quality is determined by balancing the three factors. Figure 3.1 summarizes the triple constraint.

Figure 3.1 The Triple Constraint

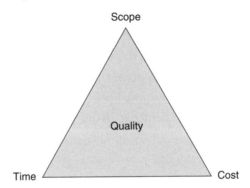

The triple constraint is a visual device that highlights the competing demands of performance, cost, and schedule. If changes are proposed that add functionality, then the project schedule will slip (become longer). It is also likely that a longer project will cost more. On the other hand, a project manager trying to shorten the schedule will probably have to add people, which will also increase the cost.

Changing any one of the scope, cost, or schedule probably impacts the other two.

SCOPE CREEP

Scope creep is the tendency for the project's requirements to grow over time. Scope creep is a common project affliction. A scope statement that is broad and imprecise is an invitation for scope creep. Most of the time, scope creep results in cost overruns and delays.

Significant scope changes can accumulate to the point where the original cost and schedule estimates are unachievable. On the other hand, given a well-defined, clear scope statement, the project team will immediately realize when extra work is being proposed. A clear scope statement is therefore essential in controlling scope creep.

It is important to realize that changes are inevitable in all projects. When combating scope creep, the project manager must be aware of when scope changes are being proposed and carefully manage their consequences. Each proposed change should be recorded and analyzed to determine the impact on the project objectives. Only after the consequences (to scope, cost, and schedule) have been analyzed should the scope change be agreed to.

The way to prevent scope creep from getting out of hand is to follow a scope management plan, which is a step-by-step process for managing changes to the project scope. This plan indicates how scope changes will be identified, how they will be integrated into the project, and what approval requirements are needed. Tracking changes in the scope management plans allows the project manager to communicate to the stakeholders how frequently and by how much the scope is changing. This is a key indicator in the stability of the project.

In combating scope creep, a key question for the project manager to ask is, "Is this a refinement or an add-on?" Refinements are desirable and necessary. Add-ons result in cost overruns and schedule slippages.

In well-run organizations, it is common to have a generic scope management plan in place so that a different plan does not have to be established for every new project. Scope management plans may contain basic or in-depth information and can be formal or informal documents, depending on the size of the project.

SCOPE DEFINITION TOOLS

Since preparation of the scope is so critical to a project's success, it needs to be thoroughly analyzed for completeness and precision. There are many tools to help the project manager with this task.

Conduct a Product Analysis

Will the project meet the organization's business needs? Product analysis includes techniques such as systems engineering and analysis, and value and function analysis. Value analysis techniques analyze performance and capabilities relative to cost. Net present value and return on investment calculations identify the value a project will bring to the organization. A function analysis determines what functionality a product will add to the company by prioritizing objectives.

Conduct a Cost/Benefit Analysis

A cost/benefit analysis helps to determine what to put into products to get out the greatest benefits. Project alternatives are assessed by estimating tangible and intangible costs and benefits. Tangible costs are the costs of making the product or the costs of completing a project. Intangible costs, also called opportunity costs, include opportunities missed by choosing one project over another. In other words, by doing Project A, what do we miss by not doing Project B?

Completing a cost/benefit analysis helps to determine whether the benefits of a project exceed the costs by a margin that is acceptable to the organization. During a cost/benefit analysis, companies typically look at both short-term and long-term benefits over the life of the project.

For example, pharmaceutical companies plan for a ten-year development cycle. This lengthy development cycle may not yield many short-term benefits, but if the company is the first to market with a new drug, the payoff is significant.

Ask for Expert Recommendations

Ask an individual who has experience with similar projects to analyze the scope. Outside experts have the advantage of being independent. While they may not understand all of the intricacies of a company and its goals, neither are they susceptible to company politics.

Identify Alternatives

Identify different approaches for completing the project. Brainstorming or "lateral thinking" can generate different, more effective approaches. Alternative approaches will have different performance requirements, costs, and schedules. Even if the alternate approaches are not chosen, their analysis will highlight assumptions and clarify technical issues.

Conduct a Stakeholder Analysis

Stakeholder analysis identifies the influence and interests of the various stakeholders by documenting their expectations. The analysis usually results in the prioritization, selection, and quantification of stakeholder needs. Unquantifiable expectations, such as customer satisfaction, may be documented to help prevent future conflict.

SCOPE ERRORS

Academics and practitioners have been collecting data for decades on the impact of errors made in the scope definition (or requirements) stage of a project. It is depressing how little progress has been made. In 1981, in a book entitled *Software Engineering Economics,* Barry Boehm said:

> If a software requirement error is detected and corrected during the plans and requirements phase, its correction is a relatively simple matter … If the same error is not corrected until the maintenance phase … the error is typically 100 times more expensive to correct.

Many studies have been conducted since then and all seem to reach the same conclusion.

Suppose the scope document has an error in it, and assume that the average cost to fix that error during the requirements analysis phase is one person for one week (one man-week). An excellent estimate of what it will cost to fix that scope error in the succeeding phases of the project is shown in figure 3.2.

Although this data refers to software projects, there is ample data from many other industries to suggest that this rule of thumb is universal.

Figure 3.2 Cost to Fix Requirements Errors

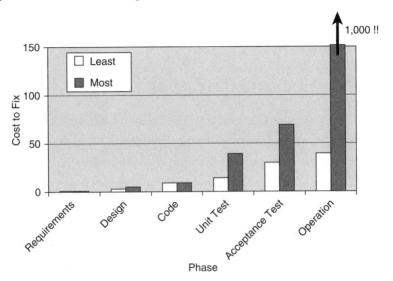

An error made in the scope definition costs 1,000 times as much to fix if not discovered until the project is deployed.

If errors in the scope occurred only rarely, then this would not be much of a problem. However, we now come to a less known, but equally interesting idea:

Scope errors are the most common errors.

In a U.S. Air Force study by F. T. Sheldon, errors were classified by source. It was found that requirements errors comprised 41 percent of the errors discovered, while logic design errors made up only 28 percent of the total error count. The combination of these two results is devastating.

Requirements errors are very common and, if not discovered, extremely expensive to fix.

What is the lesson for a project manager? Spend time on the scope. Don't rush to get the scope finished. Analyze it carefully and thoroughly—your future career may depend on it.

PROJECT MANAGEMENT IN ACTION

In December 2004, the University of Michigan and Google announced a project to digitize the university's library collection. While digitizing millions of books is a huge project, the project requirements (i.e., the scope) are quite simple—just a couple of pages. The essential features are the following:

- The collection will be searchable by Google.
- The Michigan Library will receive and own a copy of all images.
- There will be no charge for access to the library content.
- It will be possible for a user to search the full text of all the volumes digitized and to view every page of an out-of-copyright book.

There is design information included in the scope statement, e.g., what the users will see. A Google search returning results from a book in copyright will return:

- Three "snippets" of text from throughout the volume, with a "snippet" consisting of approximately three lines of content
- A count of the number of times the search term appears in the volume
- The bibliographic data associated with the book
- Information on where to buy the book or find it at a local library

The scope document also includes technical requirements, such as:

- The quality of the capture and digital files is such that the digital files are consistent with library preservation community standards for readability and best practices.
- The processes Google uses to digitally capture the books and journals are nondestructive and do not disbind library materials.

Finally, the scope includes legal issues, such as:

- The library's use of these files will be within legal and mission-oriented parameters.
- Google must work within the constraints of copyright laws.

TEST YOURSELF

Construct a scope document for a friend's 50th wedding anniversary party. It is supposed to be a well-attended party for 100 guests with a budget of $5,000.

Hint: The activities should include planning the party and the food, sending invitations, and booking the site. Remember to include all items in the scope.

KEY POINTS TO REMEMBER

- No charter, no project.
- The scope is the key document in the project—it must be complete and precise.
- The triple constraint of scope, cost, and schedule emphasizes that changing one affects the other two.
- The scope elements:
  - Project description
  - Justification or opportunity
  - Goals and objectives (SMART)
  - Deliverables
  - Milestones
  - Assumptions
  - Limits and constraints
  - The statement of work
  - Customer interface
- The statement of work (SOW) defines who is to perform what tasks.
- Scope creep is uncontrolled growth of the project.
- Scope errors are the most frequent type of project errors and the most expensive to fix.

The Work Breakdown Structure

INTRODUCTION

We saw in the previous chapter that the scope provides the well-defined, achievable goals of the project and a road map for achieving them. It defines all of the products, services, and results to be provided.

The next step of the project is to divide the scope into activities; that is, work components that can be planned, estimated, scheduled, and assigned to staff members. This is achieved through a process called decomposition—the subdivision of the scope into smaller, more manageable pieces. However, this decomposition is not arbitrary. The activities are carefully grouped into a hierarchical, deliverable-oriented decomposition called a work breakdown structure (WBS).

The reason the WBS focuses on deliverables is that they provide a solid basis for cost estimation and scheduling. The scope of the project is first divided into a few large-scale activities. Each of these is in turn decomposed into several smaller activities.

Decomposition continues with the scope being divided into smaller and smaller entities until it reaches the smallest level, at which point the activities are called work packages. Work packages may vary in size, but should be detailed enough so that the cost and schedule can be reliably estimated.

The WBS both defines and organizes the total scope. The scope is divided up, and it is continually refined by increasing detail. The WBS becomes the foundation for project planning and is one of the most important project management tools.

WHAT'S AHEAD

- What is the work break-down structure? (WBS)
- How to construct a WBS
- Why the WBS is important
- How focusing on deliverables provides a solid basis for cost estimation and scheduling
- Why the WBS is a list of activities, not things
- Decomposition of the WBS into tangible items
- The lowest level consists of work packages
- How big should work packages be?

IN THE REAL WORLD

Suppose I decide to add a garage to my house in Boston with space for two cars. The scope of the project is pretty clear—space for two cars. However, there are several ways I can accomplish this:

- A carport
- A garage next to the house
- A garage under the house

These would all meet the basic requirement of space for two cars, and each has its advantages and disadvantages, as well as its own cost and schedule. As the customer, the choice between the implementations is mine. I reject the carport option (snow in Boston!) and the digging out a garage under the house option (cost and mess!).

The next step of project management is to list the activities required to build the space for two cars. I selected an underground garage, then one of the first activities would be to dig a big hole.

The activities to be performed are described in a work breakdown structure (WBS) document. When I examine the WBS, I will see all of the proposed activities for the entire project. I will immediately be able to tell if I am getting a garage, a carport, or an underground parking spot.

DEFINING THE WBS

Creating the work breakdown structure is the process of subdividing the major deliverables and project work into smaller and more manageable components.

> ## WBS Definition
>
> The WBS is a deliverable-oriented, hierarchical decomposition of the work to be performed by the project team.

You occasionally see a WBS divided into the objects in the project. For example, the WBS for a car may be decomposed into body, transmission, engine, electrical system, etc. However, adding the proper verbs clarifies the WBS and turns the objects into activities.

The WBS identifies all deliverables required for a project and is the standard way to organize the work to be performed. To complete a WBS effectively, each deliverable is decomposed into manageable subdeliverables. Doing so helps to clarify and refine the total scope of the project.

It should be emphasized that the WBS focuses on deliverables. That way, the completion of each activity is marked by the production of a specific, easily identified entity. Deliverables also provide a solid basis for cost estimation and scheduling. The WBS is therefore a list of activities, not things.

A WBS can be set up in either graphical or outline format. Figure 4.1 shows a WBS in graphical form, which gives a visual representation of the deliverables in a treelike structure, with smaller deliverables branching out from the larger deliverables they support. This layout makes it easier to understand all of the parts of the project and how they are related, and it is therefore the form usually used in the early stages of the project.

Figure 4.1 WBS in Graphical, Tree Structured Format

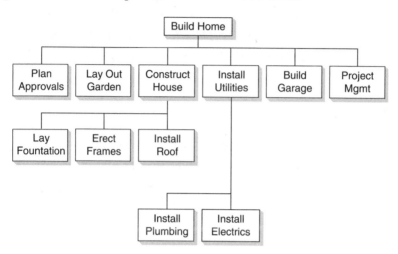

The structure of the WBS tends to grow large fairly quickly, so it is useful to divide it into self-contained subtrees and present these separately.

Figure 4.2 shows the same WBS in outline form. The first level deliverable is listed at the left, and successive levels are appropriately indented. The outline form is a practical way to list a large number of activities and deliverables or to present a very complicated WBS.

It is easy to see the drawbacks of the graphical form: it is hard to get it onto a single sheet and difficult to revise. However, it is an excellent way to communicate the higher levels to customers, management, and stakeholders. It is also an excellent tool for presenting status as the project progresses.

The graphical and outline presentation forms can be combined, which makes for an effective communication tool. For example, the higher levels can be presented in graphical form. As the decomposition proceeds, it is more effective to present the lower levels in numbered outline format, which is more suitable for technical presentations.

Sometimes the phases of a project are listed at the highest level. For example, in software development, the highest levels of the WBS are typically labeled requirements, analysis, design, code, testing, and integration. These activities reflect the phases (i.e., activities) of the software life cycle.

Figure 4.2 WBS in Outline Format

```
1.0  Build Home
        1.1  Plan Approvals
        1.2  Lay Out Garden
        1.3  Construct House
                1.3.1  Lay Foundation
                1.3.2  Erect Frames
                1.3.3  Install Roof
        1.4  Fitting Out
                1.4.1  Install Utilities
                        1.4.1.1 Install Plumbing
                        1.4.1.2 Install Electrics
                        1.4.1.3 Install Furnace
                        1.4.1.4 Install Heating Pipes
                1.4.2  Decorate
                        1.4.2.1 Paint Rooms
                        1.4.2.2 Wallpaper Rooms
                        1.4.2.3 Paint Trim
                1.4.3  Buy Appliances
        1.5  Build Garage
        1.6  Project Management
                1.6.1  Customer Reviews
                1.6.2  Customer Approvals
```

The WBS both refines and organizes the total scope. The WBS decomposition process refines the scope by dividing it into smaller pieces, thus defining the project in increasing detail. The WBS also organizes the scope by grouping the activities into manageable pieces. Creating the WBS is a part of the scope development process, and the completion of the scope is marked by the completion of the WBS.

The key to understanding the WBS is the level of breakdown. First, the WBS should only be decomposed until it makes sense. It is not necessary to break down all activities to the same level. In figure 4.2, it was decided that the "Plan Approvals" need not be divided further. Neither is it necessary to create all layers at the same time. For example, in figure 4.2, the garage breakdown has been left to a future date, when the details for the type of garage can be clarified. More detail is provided for the "Construct House" deliverable, because that is where more effort is required to communicate to the customer the exact details as envisioned at this point.

When constructing a WBS it is important to include all team members and to expect that it will take several iterations to come to an agreement. Including the team encourages everyone to think about all aspects of the project. One of the best ways to construct a WBS is to use small squares of sticky paper and just put them up on a blank wall. New WBS activities are easily created, and existing activities can be quickly moved around. Activities can be regrouped as needed and new structures can be proposed and evaluated.

The WBS also reflects organizational and developmental decisions. Since project management is an activity of the project, there should be a project management activity in the WBS. If there is a full-time, on-site project manager, with responsibility for quality control of the work and the materials, then there will be many project management activities in the WBS. One of the most important items to be included in the project management activity of the WBS is customer management, which includes creation of monthly reports, meetings, etc.

Between the higher and lower layers of the WBS, there is an intermediate level called the control account. This is a collection of work packages that can be managed together by the organization. Control accounts are often assigned to functional departments. For example, in figure 4.2, the "Erect Frames" activity can be assigned to the carpentry department, and the "Lay Out Garden" to the landscaping department.

WBS → CONTROL ACCOUNT → WORK PACKAGES

The control account supports several other bookkeeping functions: tracking of deliverables, cost estimation and planning, budgeting, accounting procedures, etc. An organization's financial reporting is typically performed at the level of the control account. For example, it makes sense that the financial reporting for all of the landscape department's activities be reported together.

CREATING A WBS

The items in the boxes of the WBS are called activities. Activities should be defined with verbs. Compare the following:

Design Garden

Garden

The first form includes a verb, which communicates valuable information. Adding the word *design* tells us that the garden is to be laid out. It also tells us that in this activity, the garden is *not* going to be dug or planted. If it were, the activity would have been described as "design, dig, and plant garden." We see that verbs are crucial in clearly and precisely communicating the activity to be completed.

Also, activities are deliverable-oriented, and we can imagine that the deliverable for the item on the left is the garden design document. We will know when the activity is completed because the design document will be delivered.

The form on the right leaves it ambiguous as to what is to be accomplished (design? digging?). Also, there is no clear deliverable, so it will be impossible to know when the activity is complete.

As another example, consider the WBS for a project to add a garage. The WBS is a deliverable-oriented decomposition, and the deliverable is the garage. However, right at the start, we have options: build it ourselves or hire someone to build it. Verbs clarify this:

Build
Garage

It is now clear to everyone (i.e., all stakeholders, including your spouse) that you are going to build the garage!

Dividing the scope into smaller and smaller work elements, or activities, is a *creative process*; there is no automated way to accomplish the breakdown of the scope into a WBS. It turns out that choosing good subsystems (i.e., the decomposition process) is quite difficult, but it helps to realize that breaking the scope into parts is a design decision. Some people are really good at design, and others are not. However, it is quite difficult to determine what makes a good breakdown and thus, a workable WBS.

One of the best ways to analyze a WBS to see if it is any good is to throw it up on the wall and let people talk about it. It is not unusual for a WBS to undergo many iterations before everyone is satisfied.

REQUIREMENTS AND DESIGN

In the beginning of a project (initiating) a preliminary scope is developed followed by a preliminary WBS. In the next phase (planning), the complete project scope is developed, followed by the updated WBS. What needs clarification is that the scope document often has two distinct stages: requirements and design.

The first step of scope development emphasizes the product's requirements. Requirements reflect the desires of the customer—what the project must do. Next comes the design stage, in which the customer's requirements are turned into a specific realization—the design. Usually, there are many designs and therefore many WBSs that can achieve the same customer requirements.

Let's return once again to the garage example, and suppose that the scope statement says that there must be space for two cars. There are several ways to accomplish this: a carport, a garage next to the house, a garage under the house, etc. These are all different design ideas that will meet the customer requirement of space for two cars. Each design has its advantages and disadvantages, as well as its own cost and schedule. The choice between the designs is the customer's, and it will reflect the climate (a carport in Boston?), cost (under the house!), etc.

Also, the detailed requirements will change depending on both the design and the high-level requirements. For example, a flat roof won't work because it will not support the snow in Boston. So the requirements and the design tend to get mixed up. It is an inherent complication of the process.

Let's not lose sight of these important distinctions:

- "Two cars" is a requirement
- "Carport" is a design choice

Now suppose we attempt to list the WBS activities. You cannot even begin until you know the type of garage selected. There will be a huge difference in WBS activities between building a garage ("Build walls, roof, etc."); building a carport ("Put some posts in the ground"); and building an underground car park ("Dig a really big hole!"). Therefore, a detailed WBS is inherently a design document.

One of the objectives of the WBS creation process is to ensure that the decomposition satisfies all of the requirements. Suppose the scope document says "the garage will keep two cars dry even in a snowstorm." (This is an example of a good scope statement because it is a precise and testable requirement.) We know that the carport design will not satisfy that requirement, so the carport implementation must be rejected. Construction of the WBS relates the requirements (what) to the design (how).

DECOMPOSING THE SCOPE

Decomposing the WBS consists of dividing the scope into manageable pieces. The fundamental idea is to successively break the scope into smaller and smaller activities, each of which results in a *tangible item*. Smaller items are easier to plan, manage, and schedule.

The process is inherently iterative. It typically takes several tries for everyone to agree on a decent WBS. By dividing up the project's scope, you break it into smaller activities and deliverables and take smaller steps toward achieving the greater whole.

The process in which the WBS is progressively elaborated is called "rolling wave planning." Work to be accomplished in the near term may be planned in much more detail than work far in the future.

Also, once you have divided up the entire scope, you are done. You should not add anything that is not included in the scope document. The Project Management Institute is very fussy about "gold-plating"—the process of adding unspecified items. This is universally frowned upon throughout the PMBOK.

Breaking deliverables into smaller deliverables has several advantages:

• Estimates for cost, time, and resources are much more accurate.

• Smaller deliverables are more manageable because it is easier to understand their progress.

- Small deliverables are more precise, resulting in fewer changes once the project begins.
- Each project deliverable can be assigned to one or two team members, resulting in greater accountability.
- The project manager can measure the project's performance by measuring the completion of the smaller deliverables.
- Controlling the project is easier, since you are dealing with smaller pieces of the overall project.

The major deliverables are decomposed down to the smallest possible element that can be *reasonably planned and managed*. When doing so, it is important to remember that every deliverable should be defined in terms of a tangible, verifiable entity. For example, for the house's plumbing system, one of the smallest activities you could identify might be "install faucets." The activity is well specified because there is a clear deliverable—working faucets. Also, it is clear when this activity is complete: either the faucets work and water comes out, or they don't.

Deliverables should be precise and easy to understand. In the planning phase to come, they will be sequenced, scheduled, and budgeted. Also, each deliverable must be assigned to an appropriate individual or group on the project team, who is then held accountable for its completion.

A work breakdown structure is a fundamental part of a project for the following reasons:

- It finalizes the scope of a project. Any work not listed in the WBS is outside the scope of the project.
- It is the primary input to the network, scheduling, and budgeting processes.
- It affects the accuracy of the cost and schedule estimates, which depends directly on the quality of the WBS.
- It allows the assignment of work responsibilities to specific team members.

- It allows the monitoring of progress of the project as a whole, since each deliverable is a measurable unit of work.

- It allows the project manager to track time, cost, and performance throughout the project.

- It establishes the basis for earned value status-reporting procedures.

WORK PACKAGES

As deliverables are broken into smaller pieces, they become more detailed. There are three types of deliverables in a WBS. High-level deliverables give a broad overview of the project. For example, when a house is built, a high-level deliverable could be "Build Roof." Notice the verb, which distinguishes the activity from something like "Purchase Prebuilt Roof."

High-level deliverables are summarizations of the subordinate work packages. Summary deliverables are important because they communicate the high-level deliverables of the project to the stakeholders. When a house is built, summary deliverables might include Build Roof, Construct Framing, Add Exterior Shingles, and Build Chimney. In a status meeting, it would be easy for the project manager to communicate the precise status of such deliverables (i.e., it is easy to see if the chimney is finished).

The second, middle level of the WBS contains the control accounts, which are used to manage the finances for the project. The third and lowest level items in the WBS are the work packages, which are the smallest manageable units that can effectively be planned, budgeted, scheduled, executed, and controlled.

The lowest level of the WBS contains work packages.

In the garage example, a work package might be "Paint Garage." This activity has enough detail that its cost can be estimated, it can be scheduled, and the responsibility for its completion can be assigned to a single person. Several painters may work on the activity, but there will only be one person who is accountable for the performance of the painting (quality of the work, cost, and schedule).

> Work packages should be written as actions.

Each work package is described in a document called a WBS dictionary. This typically includes all the relevant sections of the scope and SOW, which result in a list of activities to be accomplished. The work package details the defined deliverables and the schedule for their production. Other relevant information might include the responsible party, the cost and schedule, applicable contractual information, and any technical references that apply.

The full collection of work packages gives the project manager a sound basis for estimating and planning the project. Also, as the project proceeds, its progress can be assessed by the completion of the deliverables associated with the work packages. If a work package is not completed on time, a smaller work package is less likely to be as late. A very large work package might get into trouble and the project manager may not know about it. With smaller work packages, it is easier to identify when corrective action is needed to keep the project on track.

WORK PACKAGE SIZE

A common problem is that work packages are left too large, making them difficult to control. When a work package is an unmanageable size, it can take longer than planned to complete. There are some simple guidelines that help keep work packages to a reasonable size. A common rule of thumb for the size of a work package is the following:

> The effort in a work package should be one to two people
> for one to two weeks.

If a problem occurs during the execution of a work package of this size, then the worst that can happen is that it will become clear after week two that there is a problem.

Another common practice is making sure a work package does not take longer to complete than the length of time between status reports. For example, if you hold weekly status meetings, it is useful if the individual work packages do not take longer than one week to complete. In that case, each week there are a specific number of work packages that should have been completed, and during a status meeting it will be clear which work packages are not complete. Immediate corrective action can be taken.

For every work package, the progress should be easy to track and accountability should be easy to assign. If this is not the case, the work package is probably too large or the deliverable is not clearly defined.

WHEN IS A WORK PACKAGE FULLY DECOMPOSED?

The following characteristics help to determine when a work package has been fully decomposed:

- At any time, the project manager must be able to gain an *accurate* estimate of when the deliverable has been (or will be) completed.
- The deliverable must have clearly defined beginning and end criteria.
- The end of a deliverable represents a physical accomplishment, which is the product or service.
- The project manager must be able to develop reliable cost and time estimates for each work package.
- Each work package should be independent so that once work has begun, it can continue without additional input or without being interrupted.
- Once a work package is closed, any additional related work requires a new work package.

EXISTING WBS

Keep in mind that a WBS may already exist for your project. Although each project is unique, there are frequently enough similarities between projects that organizations keep a standard WBS on file that can be used as a template. Using a WBS template can save time when planning a project.

THE WBS IN ACTION

Since the five PMI project phases are activities, we can use them as the basis for a WBS. Figure 4.3 shows the WBS for a project that follows that kind of structure.

Figure 4.3 WBS for Vista Migration Project

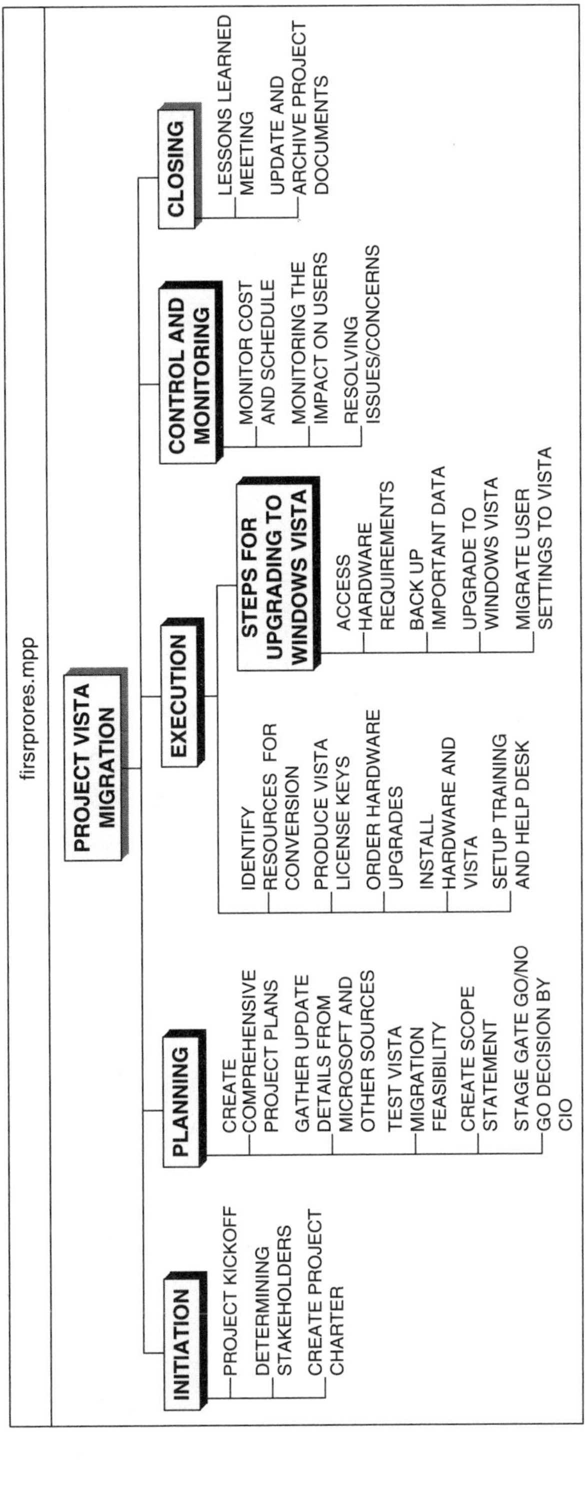

TEST YOURSELF

Create a WBS for the 50th anniversary party using the scope document you created in chapter 3. Create a high-level WBS only for the entire party and a detailed breakdown for the party preplanning.

KEY POINTS TO REMEMBER

- The WBS is a deliverable-oriented decomposition of the scope.
- The WBS should be clear and easy to understand.
- WBS activities require verbs to clarify them.
- All activities listed in the WBS should produce a deliverable.
- Deliverables listed in the WBS should be tangible, making it easy to recognize when they are complete.
- The lowest levels of the WBS tree are the work packages, whose size is one to two people for one to two weeks.
- Work packages should be assignable to responsible individuals.
- Each work package should be a direct subset of a summary deliverable, and each summary deliverable should be a direct subset of a high-level deliverable.

The Network

INTRODUCTION

In the previous chapter, we developed the WBS, which is a list of activities. To make a network, we add two ideas: the order in which the activities must be performed and the length of time it will take to complete each activity. Adding these two simple concepts to the WBS will allow us to create a schedule for the entijre project.

WHAT'S AHEAD

- What is a network diagram?
- Why do I need a network diagram?
- How do you construct a network diagram?

- What is the critical path?
- Why is the critical path important?

IN THE REAL WORLD

You are having a small dinner party for friends. Before you start, you do a little planning and make a list of the activities to be completed:

- Shop for ingredients
- Cook food
- Set the table
- Eat

These activities cannot be completed in a random order. The shopping must be completed before the cooking can start. However, we can set the table while cooking the food. And of course, we can't start eating until the both the food is cooked and the table is set.

We have established an order for the activities. More important, we have also specified their dependencies. For example, eating requires that both of the activities leading up to it must be completed. We have not just specified the order, but a more subtle relation about both of the activities that precede eating.

If we add up the times for all of the activities, we will not get the time required for the entire project. This is because setting the table and cooking can be done in parallel. So how do we find out how long the project will take? Or put another way, when do we go shopping in order to finish eating in time to go to the movies at 7 P.M.?

KEY CONCEPTS

We begin with this simple example, which contains everything you need to know about networks. Networks can get pretty complicated, but even the most sophisticated only contain the features in our simple example. Once you have mastered this example, you can analyze any network!

The result of developing the network is a schedule for the entire project. A few simple rules will allow us to determine how long the project will take, i.e., the schedule.

However, even more important than the schedule is the critical path. This is the path that determines the schedule, so the activities on the critical path become the most important. Once we have the critical path (or paths, as there may be more than one), project management decisions get so much simpler.

Remember, there is no concept of time in the WBS—it is just a list of activities. To construct a network, the first thing to be done is to take the list of activities in the WBS and establish their dependencies: Which activities must be completed before others can begin? For example, you have to finish buying rice before you can start cooking it. This is called activity sequencing.

We also must determine how long each activity will take. Adding the length of time an activity will take to complete will allow us to create a schedule for the entire project. We will assume for the purposes of this chapter that the time estimate for each activity is known. We will ignore for now the estimation process and just concentrate on the construction of the network.

COOKING DINNER

Let's return to the simple example of having a small dinner party for friends. We made a list of the activities to be completed:

- Shop for ingredients
- Cook food
- Set the table
- Eat

We need two things to turn this list of activities into a network: a sequence of activities (i.e., the order in which they must occur) and a time estimate for each of the activities. The sequence is defined by determining the predecessors for each activity. To do that we construct the following table:

Table 5.1 Activity Sequences and Time Estimates

Identification	Description	Predecessors	Duration
A	Shop for ingredients	None	2
B	Cook food	A	3
C	Set the table	A	1
D	Eat	B, C	4

First the activities are identified by a letter. There are many ways to do this, and we have simply chosen to identify them as A, B, C, and D. One can also number them according to the WBS hierarchy. Each activity also has a duration, which tells us how long the activity will take to complete. In the planning stage of the project, these are estimates. Later on, these may change to actual times as activities are completed.

Shopping can be started at any time, so activity A has no predecessors. In making the shopping list, we realize that we are out of napkins, so we cannot start to lay the table until we have bought some more. Therefore, neither cooking (B) nor laying the table (C) can start until the shopping (A) is finished. Also, we cannot begin to eat until the cooking is finished and the table is completely laid. All of these relations are indicated in the table in the "predecessors" column. The last line of the table is read as follows: Activity D cannot begin until both activities B and C are finished, and activity D takes four hours.

Using the precedent relations, we can now construct the following diagram:

Figure 5.1 Network Diagram

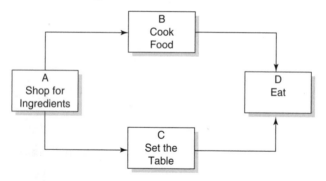

The arrows in figure 5.1 have a very specific meaning. The arrow from activity A to activity B means:

> Activity B cannot start until activity A is completely finished.

This is called a finish-to-start constraint. Earlier, we said that we had run out of napkins, so the table could not be laid until the shopping was finished. This is indicated in figure 5.1 by the arrow from A to C. Activity C (set the table) cannot start until activity A (shop for ingredients) has been completed.

There are two arrows going into activity D. This means that eating cannot start until *both* the cooking is finished *and* the table laying is finished. We emphasize the precise meaning of the arrows: the activity at the head of the arrow cannot start until the activity at the tail has completely finished.

CALCULATING EARLIEST FINISH (FORWARD PASS)

If we start the shopping at noon, when will we finish eating? This is an important question—it asks "how long is our project?" To answer the question, we use the following notation. Each activity is described by the following box:

Table 5.2 Activity Parameters

Earliest Start	ID	Earliest Finish
Slack	Description	Slack
Latest Start	Duration	Latest Finish

Shopping (A) is the first activity. We can fill in the identity (A), the description (shop for ingredients), and the duration (two hours). The earliest that the first activity—the shopping—can start is at time zero. Therefore, we put a zero in the top left-hand box for activity A. The first activity generally has an earliest start at time = zero.

Table 5.3 Forward Pass Parameters for Activity A

0	A	2
	Shop for Ingredients	
	2	

If the earliest start for the shopping (A) is at time zero, and its duration is two hours, then the earliest time that the shopping can be completed is at time 2. We therefore put 2 in the top right-hand box. Therefore, the earliest finish for activity A is 2.

We now discuss activity B (cook food). In figure 5.1, there is an arrow from A to B, and the arrow means that activity B cannot start until activity A has been completed (cooking cannot start until shopping is complete). Since the earliest finish for A is 2, the earliest start for B is also 2.

If the earliest start for the cooking (B) is at time 2, and its duration is 3 hours, then the earliest time that the cooking can be completed is at time 5. We therefore put 5 in the top right-hand box, denoting the fact that the earliest finish for activity B is 5.

Table 5.4 Forward Pass Parameters for Activity B

2	B	5
	Shop for Ingredients	
	3	

This shows the power of the definition of the "finish-to-start" arrows. It allows us to connect the activities. We can now complete the diagram for C and D:

Figure 5.2 Completed Forward Pass

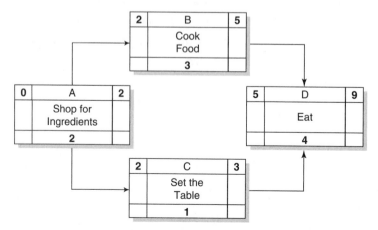

The arrow from A to C means that activity C (set the table) can only begin once activity A (shopping) has been completed. Since the earliest finish for A is 2, the earliest start for C is 2. This is indicated in the top left box of activity C in figure 5.2. Since the earliest start for C is at time 2, and its duration is one hour, the earliest time that C can be completed is at time 3. We therefore put 3 in the top right-hand box, denoting the fact that the earliest finish for activity C is 3.

There are two arrows going into activity D (eat). The arrow from B to D means that activity D cannot begin until B has finished. Similarly, the arrow from C to D means that activity D cannot begin until C has finished. Therefore, activity D cannot begin until *both* B and C have been completed.

The meaning of the arrows allows us to compute the earliest start for activity D. Eating has to wait until both "cook food" and "set the table" have been completed. The earliest that eating can start, therefore, is after whichever activity (B or C) is the last to finish. The earliest finish for B is 5, and for C is 3. Since the last to finish is B, the earliest start for D is at time 5.

When two arrows go into an activity, it is called a merge activity. The merge activity cannot start until both preceding activities are complete, so the earliest start time of the merge activity is the latest of the preceding activities.

The duration for D is 4, and so the earliest time that D can finish is at time 9. Since D is the final activity, we have arrived at the earliest finish for the entire project: time 9.

This completes the forward pass. The only complication was that when two arrows entered an activity, we took the *latest* of the earliest finish times as the earliest start time for the next activity to start. Since B will take longer than C, there is some spare time between the finish of C and the beginning of D.

The power of the forward pass is now clear. The forward pass determines the earliest finish for the entire project. If we start shopping at noon, the earliest we can expect to finish eating is at 9 P.M.

CALCULATING LATEST START (BACKWARD PASS)

We now ask the question, "What is the latest finish for the project?" The answer typically depends on customer's wishes. If we wanted to go to a movie at 9 P.M., we might specify that we need to finish dinner by 8 P.M. In the above diagram, it is easy to see that we have a problem, because the earliest finish is 9 P.M.

When activity times are estimated, the effect of adding them together in the network diagram is generally not known. For example, we estimated that "cook food" would take three hours. We cannot change this; it is our best estimate for the time to complete the activity. Therefore, it is not unusual for the earliest finish time for the entire project (calculated from the forward pass) to come out to be later than the desired finish time for the entire project.

Let's impose the condition that the longest duration for the project is nine hours. This means that activity D (eating) has a latest finish of 9. What usually goes in the lower right box for the last activity (in this case, D) is the customer's desired ending time for the project. We put 9 in the bottom right-hand box for activity D.

Table 5.5 Backward Pass Parameters for Activity D

	D	
	Eat	
5	4	9

If the latest finish for the "eat" activity (D) is 9, and its duration is four hours, then the latest start for eating is at time 5 (9 − 4 = 5). We therefore put 5 in the bottom left-hand box for activity D, its latest start. We can now complete the backward pass, which is shown in figure 5.3.

Figure 5.3 Completed Backward Pass

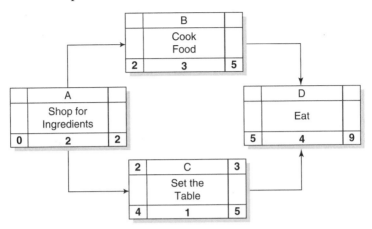

D can start as soon as both B and C have finished (this is the meaning of the arrows from B and C to D). Therefore, since the latest start for D is 5, the latest finish for both B and C is also 5. For B, the duration is 3, and since the latest finish is 5, the latest start is 2 (5 − 3 = 2). Similarly, the latest start for C is 4 (5 − 1 = 4).

The arrows from A to B and A to C mean that activities B and C can begin once A is completed. B has the *earliest* of the latest starts of B and C. Therefore, since the latest start for B is 2, the latest finish for A must also be 2. (If the latest start for C (4) were inserted for the latest finish for A, then this would violate the condition that B's latest start is 2. In that case the latest finish for A would be 4, and that is after the latest start for B, which is 2.)

For A, the duration is 2, and since the latest finish is 2, the latest start is 0 (2 − 2 = 0). Since A is the first activity, we have arrived at the latest start for the entire project: The latest start for the project is at time 0. This completes the backward pass.

The only complication was that when two arrows came out of an activity, we took the *earliest* of the latest finish times as its latest start time.

We could have insisted that because we want to go to the movies at 9 P.M., the latest finish for the project should be 8 P.M. In which case, we would put 8 for the latest finish for activity D (the lower right-hand box).

The same process would lead to the latest start for activity A = −1. This simply means that to finish at 8 P.M., we need to start an hour earlier.

CRITICAL PATH AND SLACK

We now come to one of the most important concepts in project management—the critical path. In figure 5.4, the path A, B, D is the longest path through the network and so represents the shortest time that the project can be completed. The path A, B, D is called the critical path.

Figure 5.4 The Critical Path and Slack

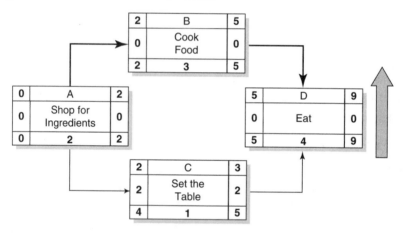

The critical path is the longest path through the network.

The critical path is the shortest time in which the project can be completed.

The activities A, B, and D are critical because if anything delays any one of them, the entire project will be delayed. If the shopping takes three hours rather than the two hours that was planned, the eating will not finish until one hour later than scheduled.

Activity C does not lie on the critical path, so it can be delayed without affecting the project schedule. If setting the table begins as soon as the shopping is completed, even if it takes an extra hour, it will not delay the project. Activity C is said to have some slack. The slack for each task is calculated as follows:

$$\text{Slack} = \text{Latest Finish} - \text{Earliest Finish (LF} - \text{EF)}$$

or

$$\text{Slack} = \text{Latest Start} - \text{Earliest Start (LS} - \text{ES)}$$

The easy way to remember the above formulas is indicated in figure 5.4 by the arrow to the right of the diagram: one subtracts the top number from the bottom number. The values for the slack are shown in figure 5.4. For example, for activity D, the latest finish, LF, is 9 and the earliest finish, EF, is 9, so the slack is LF − EF = 9 − 9 = 0. Similarly, the latest start, LS, is 5 and the earliest start, ES, is 5, so the slack is LS − ES = 5 − 5 = 0.

All of the activities on the critical path have the *least slack* in common. In figure 5.4, the least slack occurs for the path with zero slack. The critical path does not always have zero slack. In the example where we wish to go to the movies at 8 P.M., the path with least slack will be the path with slack = −1. The critical path will still be A, B, D; the activities will just have slack = −1. The formal definition of the critical path is:

> The critical paths are the paths that have the least slack in common.

Note that there may be more than one critical path. If the duration for activity C were 3, then there would be two critical paths: A, B, D and A, C, D.

Activity C has a slack = 2, so the "set the table" activity can be started up to two hours later and still not delay the eating. Of course, if activity C is delayed by more than two hours, it will now be on the critical path. If we forgot the napkins on the shopping trip and only realized at the last minute that we have to go back to the store, then activity C may well end up on the critical path and maybe even delay the meal and therefore, the project.

Warning:

A *task* is the word that Microsoft Project uses for an activity—tasks are essentially equivalent to activities as we have defined them. The word *task* is not used in the PMBOK.

MILESTONES

Milestones, or events, are markers on the project network diagrams that indicate important points in the project schedule. Milestones are important points in time, such as the completion of an activity and its deliverable (e.g., the completion of a document, the delivery of a subsystem, the completion of a quality review, etc.). Milestones can also denote important project management activities, such as customer meetings and management reviews.

Milestones have zero duration.

Milestones can be indicated on the network diagram. Although milestones may appear along the critical path, they do not affect the flow of a project. The activity or work to complete a milestone, however, may be on the critical path. Presentations to customers and upper management are usually clearer when presented in terms of milestones. This is because milestones represent the completion of specific activities. Also, presenting network diagrams in terms of milestones makes them less cluttered and easier to understand.

MANAGING THE CRITICAL PATH

By far the most important feature of any network diagram is its critical path. It is not at all unusual for the critical path to change during a project. Activities may be completed sooner or later than originally planned. As soon as any change occurs, the project manager should immediately check the impact on the critical path.

The critical path typically includes only a small fraction of the activities in a project. This is useful, since it means the project manager can better prioritize management decisions to ensure the critical path is not adversely affected.

Finally, one can roll up the noncritical activities. That is, a whole noncritical branch of the network can be lumped together as a single entity for management purposes. Of course, if any of those noncritical activities are late, then their impact on the critical path must be carefully assessed. Many late activities on a noncritical path can quickly turn it into a critical path.

MORE ACTIVITY SEQUENCING RELATIONSHIPS

There are different kinds of activity relationships:

- Predecessor activities
- Successor activities
- Concurrent activities
- Merge activities
- Burst activities

Predecessor Activities

Predecessor activities must *finish* before immediately following activities can begin. (A is the predecessor to B in figure 5.1.)

Successor Activities

Successor activities follow immediately after other activities. (B is the successor to A in figure 5.1.)

Concurrent Activities

Concurrent, or parallel, activities can be worked on at the same time. This often shortens the duration of the project. In figure 5.1, activities B and C are concurrent—cooking and setting the table can be performed in parallel.

Merge Activities

Merge activities have at least two preceding activities on which they depend. In figure 5.1, activity D is a merge activity (B and C merge into D).

Burst Activities

Burst activities have at least two succeeding activities on which they depend. In figure 5.1, activity A is a burst activity (B and C burst from A).

DEPENDENCIES

Dependencies dictate when or how an activity must be performed. There are three types of dependencies:

• Mandatory dependencies
• Discretionary dependencies
• External dependencies

Mandatory Dependencies

Mandatory dependencies are restrictions specific to one or more activities. A mandatory dependency may require one activity (A, shopping) to be completed before another can begin (B, cooking). For example, when building a house, the foundation must be finished before the walls can be erected. Mandatory dependencies never change. Another name for mandatory dependencies is hard logic.

Discretionary Dependencies

Discretionary dependencies are preferred ways of doing the project. They can change as priorities change, because there may be multiple ways to complete an activity. For example, the project manager may decide that the activity of setting the table may be accomplished "just in time," in which case the table is set just before eating begins. On the other hand, the project manager may decide that the table should be set as soon as possible, i.e., as soon as the napkins arrive (shopping is completed).

Team members may pick the discretionary dependency that produces the most desirable outcome for the project. For example, setting the table early may keep the project manager happy. Discretionary dependencies are also called soft logic.

Both mandatory and discretionary dependencies should be used with care, since they can affect the sequence of activities for the entire project. Assumptions involved should be documented because the justification for the assumptions may change as the project evolves.

External Dependencies

External dependencies are restrictions that result from activities outside the project itself. Usually, neither the project manager nor team members can control external dependencies. External dependencies typically include such things as the following:

- Waiting for town approval of building plans
- Waiting for deliverables from subcontractors or other projects
- Waiting for executive approval for capital acquisitions

THE SCHEDULE

One of the key roles of a project manager is schedule management. Effective schedule management ensures that projects are completed on time and helps keep the project from going over budget. This requires identifying and managing the most efficient path to project completion. The following table summarizes the key steps in schedule management.

Table 5.6 Steps in Schedule Management

Activity Definition	From the WBS, identify all of the activities required to produce all of the project's deliverables.
Activity Sequencing	Identify the order of the activities and their dependencies.

Activity Resource Estimating	Estimate the type and quantity of resources needed to complete each activity.
Activity Duration Estimating	Estimate the time needed to complete each activity.
Schedule Development	Analyze the sequences, durations, resources, and constraints to produce a schedule (the network diagram)
Schedule Control	Consider the factors that could alter the schedule (risks, resources contention, scope creep, etc.) and manage the changes to the project schedule.

One of the best ways to manage the project schedule is to create a network diagram and enter it into project management software. Most modern software packages make it quite easy to create the network diagram, so there really is no excuse for not to using them.

LEADS AND LAGS

The classic situation where a lag is used is in purchasing an item. Suppose you decide to buy a widget and the delivery time is two weeks. The time estimate for the "Buy Widget" activity might be four hours (the time it would take to fill out the purchase request form, get signatures, etc.). Therefore, the duration for the "Buy Widget" activity should be 4. However, the entire process takes two weeks, during which time no work is being performed, and you are simply waiting. To properly explain this in the network diagram, you introduce a lag into the buying activity:

Figure 5.5 A Lag

The time estimate for the "Buy Widget" activity is four hours. The "Test Widget" activity cannot start until after the lag period (say two weeks) has finished. More formally:

> In a finish-to-start dependency, a lag is the time between the finish of a predecessor activity in a network diagram and the start of its successor activity.

A lead says that an activity can begin early. (It can be thought of as a negative lag.) For example, in the preparation of a document, you might allow editors in the proofing department to start work a week early on a draft, before the document is formally completed (i.e., delivered). This is a risky action. The benefit of the schedule compression that might accrue must be balanced against the risk that the editors might have to re-edit some of the document.

Leads and lags affect the timing of activities and so affect the critical path. In fact, they make the calculation of a critical path a bit tricky. While software packages can handle them correctly, the resulting critical path may not be easy to understand.

LOOPS AND CONDITIONAL BRANCHES

A document with several parts which requires multiple drafts may be considered as an example of a project that could use loops in the sequence of activities. Suppose the first chapter is written and delivered—the activity is complete (A). The next chapter is written and delivered (activity B). Finally, the last chapter is written and delivered (activity C). See figure 5.6.

The next activity is to review the first chapter and create a second draft. This might be considered as a loop in the network diagram. That is, activity A is being re-executed. Such loops are not allowed in network diagrams. The arrow from C to A in figure 5.6 is considered illegal:

A much better way to describe the activities is the following:

- Write chapter 1
- Write chapter 2
- Write chapter 3
- Edit chapter 1
- Edit chapter 2
- Edit chapter 3

Since the activities of writing and editing have different skills and schedules, they can be assigned to different staff. So it is probably a much better
option not to use the loop.

Figure 5.6 An Illegal Loop

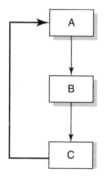

A conditional branch is one that has an "if" statement in it. An activity
is completed "if something happens." Both loops and conditional branches tend to complicate the network. If you really want to include looping
of activities and branches, a method called graphical evaluation and review technique (GERT) can be used. Typically, both loops and conditional
branches complicate the reading of network diagrams and confuse the
readers more than they help.

AOA AND AON

Two approaches can be used to describe project networks: activity-on-
node (AON) and activity-on-arrow (AOA). The diagrams in this chapter
all used AON. In practice, AON has come to dominate most projects. AON
is also called the precedence diagramming method (PDM) and is used by
most project management software packages.

In the activity-on-arrow (AOA) approach, activities are denoted
by the arrows, so that if figure 5.1 is rewritten in terms of AOA, it
becomes:

Figure 5.7 Activity on Arrow Representation of Figure 5.1

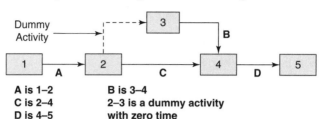

A is 1–2   B is 3–4
C is 2–4   2–3 is a dummy activity
D is 4–5   with zero time

In an AOA diagram, most of the activities are simply denoted as arrows labeled by numbered nodes. For example, activity A (shopping) is "1–2," as it goes from node 1 to node 2. The complication that occurs in an AOA diagram is the need for dummy activities. Activity B (cooking) is "5–4," and activity C (set table) is "2–4." In order to designate that B cannot start until A is finished, the dummy activity "2–3" (dotted line) is added to the network.

Some analysts claim that the AOA form is easier to read and draw. However, the addition of the dummy activities tends to make AOA more difficult to understand and construct.

THE NETWORK IN ACTION

The Vista case study deals with an organization upgrading computers from XP to Vista Business Edition. The activities in each of the five process groups (initiation, planning, executing, monitoring and controlling, and closing), along with their duration, are shown in table 5.7.

The activities in table 5.7 are shown in bar chart format in figure 5.8.

Table 5.7 Activities for the Project Vista Case Study

INITIATION	3days
PROJECT KICKOFF	1d
DETERMINING STAKEHOLDERS	1d
CREATE PROJECT CHARTER	1d

PLANNING	7d
CREATE COMPREHENSIVE PROJECT PLANS	2d
GATHER UPGRADE DETAILS FROM MICROSOFT AND OTHER SOURCES	2d
TEST VISTA MIGRATION FEASIBILITY	2d
CREATE SCOPE STATEMENT	1d
STAGE GATE GO/NO GO DECISION BY CIO	0d
EXECUTION	17d
IDENTIFY RESOURCES FOR CONVERSION	1d
PRODUCE VISTA LICENSE KEYS	1d
ORDER HARDWARE UPGRADES	1d
INSTALL HARDWARE AND VISTA	3d
SET UP TRAINING AND HELP DESK	1d
STEPS FOR UPGRADING TO WINDOWS VISTA	10d
ACCESS HARDWARE REQUIREMENTS	2d
BACK UP IMPORTANT DATA	2d
UPGRADE TO WINDOWS VISTA	5d
MIGRATE USER SETTINGS TO VISTA	1d
CONTROL AND MONITORING	3d
MONITOR COST AND SCHEDULE	1d
MONITORING THE IMPACT ON USERS	1d
RESOLVING ISSUES/CONCERNS	1d
CLOSING	2d
LESSONS LEARNED MEETING	1d
UPDATE AND ARCHIVE PROJECT DOCUMENTS	1d

Figure 5.8 Bar Chart for Vista Case Study

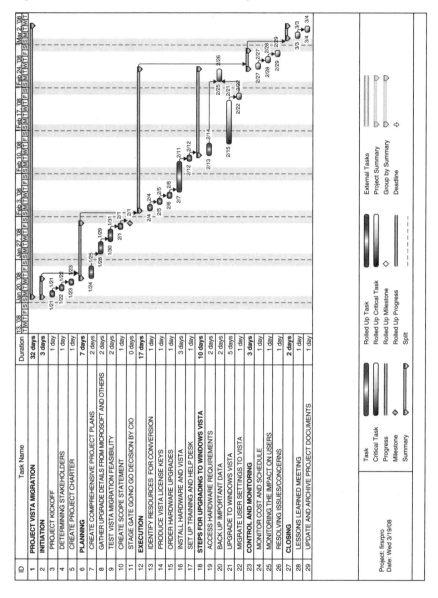

TEST YOURSELF

Consider the following table of activities:

Activity	Predecessor	Duration (days)
Start	None	None
A	Start	4
B	Start	9
C	A	6
D	A, B	8
E	C, D	4
F	B, D	2
G	E, F	5
End	G	None

1. Draw the network diagram with forward and backward passes.

2. Which activities are on the critical path?

3. If the customer wants to have the project finished in 24 days, what would you recommend?

KEY POINTS TO REMEMBER

- From the scope and WBS, list the sequence of activities (their order) and a time estimate for their completion.
- The forward pass gives the earliest time for completion of the project.
- The backward pass gives the latest start of the project.
- The critical path is the longest path through the project.
- The critical path is the shortest time in which the project can be completed.
- Milestones have zero duration.
- All decisions should be assessed to determine their impact on the critical path.

Project Execution, Monitoring, and Control

INTRODUCTION

It is ironic that a project manager does not have much to do on the project itself: the project manager manages. However, the project manager must be in complete control of the project and has a long list of responsibilities, the most important of which are control of the scope (what), the schedule (when), and the cost (how much).

WHAT'S AHEAD

- How the external company environment affects the project

- The importance of managing stakeholders

- The strengths and weaknesses of functional, matrix, and projectized organizations

- How to use the critical path to manage the project

- The importance of acquiring and managing staff

- How to decrease the time to complete a project

IN THE REAL WORLD

A manager from another project, Jenn, comes into your office and asks if she can borrow Bill for a few weeks. She desperately needs an analyst with Bill's skills for a critical activity. What do you do?

Well, the first step is pretty easy; it's the implementation that is hard. You get out your plan with the critical path on it, and look to find out what Bill is working on. If Bill is not working on an activity on the critical path, then you can breathe a sigh of relief. You can lend Bill to Jenn! You are a team player, and Jenn will owe you a big favor.

On the other hand, if Bill is working on a critical activity on your project, then things are a bit trickier. If you really want to cooperate, then the best thing to do is to ask Jenn if you can get back to her in an hour or two, in which time you can figure out what to do. First, you must find someone who has skills similar to Bill's who is not working on a critical activity. You now have a couple of choices: 1) use the new person to replace Bill, and lend Bill to Jenn, or 2) suggest to Jenn that you have found a person with similar skills whom she can borrow.

The key is that by examining the critical path for your project, you can decide which actions will have the best impact on your project. This approach applies not only to staffing decisions, but to everything! Any time a change is required, first check the impact on the critical path.

KEY CONCEPTS

Project managers spend almost all of their time managing the project. There are two aspects to this:

1. Executing
2. Monitoring and controlling

It is ironic that a project manager does not have much to do on the project itself—the project manager manages. In the execution phase, the project manager only has responsibility for a few activities. The assignments the project manager does have, however, are vital: the acquisition and supervision of the project team, managing the relations with the company, and coping with the demands of the stakeholders.

In the monitoring and controlling phase, the project manager has a catalog of responsibilities. Primarily, the project manager controls the scope, the schedule, and the cost, and one method of focusing on these is to identify, track, and evaluate risks. However, there are many other responsibilities, including collecting, measuring, and disseminating information; ensuring that changes are carefully controlled; accepting deliverables; monitoring conformance to standards; and managing contractual relationships.

THE COMPANY ENVIRONMENT

A project manager must create a positive environment for the project, both internally and externally. The external environment encompasses everything outside the project, such as:

- The parent organization, including upper management
- Organizational assets, including lessons learned, policies, and procedures
- Enterprise environmental factors, including organizational culture, existing staff, company tools, and technologies
- The political environment, including government policies, tax incentives, etc.
- The business climate, including access to funds
- The geographical setting, including environmental issues
- Social commitments, including benefits and working conditions

An important aspect of the external environment is the business need for the project. It is crucial that the project manager understands the reason for the project, as viewed from outside. The desire for the project may arise from factors such as a technological advance, a market demand, a training deficiency, or a new legal or government regulation.

The business need must be clearly established and documented. If the need disappears, the project will also. A project manager must always be ready to defend the project and articulate why it is the best solution among the competing proposals. The business world is constantly evolving, and this affects the desire for the end product, as well as its functionality. Stakeholder opinions and desires evolve also, changing the rationale for the project and the priorities of its functions. Project managers must be on the lookout for any risks to the relevance of the project.

The internal project environment influences the attitude of the team members and encourages them to succeed in producing a quality product. The project manager has more control over the internal environment and should work to foster the following:

- A corporate culture that acknowledges and appreciates the efforts of team members
- Good working relationships among team members
- Open communications between the project manager and the team
- An environment of trust
- A willingness to take risks
- Recognition of efforts and achievements

MANAGING STAKEHOLDERS

A stakeholder is defined as any individual, group, or organization actively involved in the project or an entity whose interests may be affected by the project. Stakeholders have varying levels of authority, and their influence changes over time. Formal stakeholders typically include the customer, the parent organization (including upper management), and the project team. More informal stakeholders include anyone affected by the project's end result, such as end users, training departments, community groups, etc. Other stakeholders may simply need to feel appreciated or consulted throughout the project. Project managers should adjust their efforts to meet stakeholders' needs according to their level of influence.

Locating everyone with a stake in the project and clearly defining all of their expectations is difficult and time-consuming, but failing to do so can lead to delays and overruns, and even disasters. Managing stakeholder expectations reduces conflict over competing requirements and establishes unambiguous acceptance criteria for project deliverables.

Stakeholders have varying levels of influence on a project, but they all have specific requirements they want included. The project manager must strive to meet those needs and decide the best way for their desires to be fulfilled. Not meeting stakeholder expectations is a major risk factor. For example, ignoring a stakeholder's request in the beginning of a project runs the risk of failing an acceptance test at the end by not meeting a requirement. Managing the stakeholder's expectations is a key role for the project manager.

ORGANIZATIONAL STYLES

The project's parent organization significantly affects how a project manager approaches the project. Organizations typically assign projects in one of three ways:

- Dedicated project teams, sometimes called projectized
- Functional projects
- Matrix organizations, with varying forms such as strong or weak

A project manager inherits the organizational structure, so it is important to understand the role of projects in the organization, the different types of structures in which projects exist, and the challenges that will arise in each of those structures.

Dedicated Project Teams (Projectized)

Many organizations derive most of their revenue from projects (e.g., construction firms, movie makers, information technology companies, and government contractors). Such companies are organized so that each project is a separate, self-contained unit. In this projectized setup, the project team tends to have considerable freedom and may or may not use the administrative and financial resources of the parent organization.

Some companies set up individual project structures in special circumstances, and these are called "skunk works." Separated projects are often viewed with suspicion and suspected of getting preferential treatment.

The project team can either adopt or reject the organization's values, beliefs, and expectations. For example, the parent organization may expect employees to work from 8 A.M. to 5 P.M. If the project requires long days and weekends, the project manager might decide to give team members occasional days off to make up for the extra work. A project-based organization may also institute different reward systems to promote teamwork rather than individual achievements. Such situations can cause conflict with other company employees who may regard it as special treatment for project team members.

Functional Projects

A second option is to assign the project to one of the existing functional divisions of the organization. Generally, the project is assigned to the functional department with the most expertise and the most resources and which is the most supportive in implementing the project, and the most likely to ensure the project's success.

For example, software projects are typically assigned to the information systems department. Suppose a manufacturing company wants to improve their inventory system. They may put a team together and charge them with the responsibility of defining and implementing the project. The team members stay associated with their own departments and come together to coordinate the job of the project. One of the team members might be assigned the job of chair of the committee and would be responsible for the objectives, milestones, and deliverables. In project management language, the chair is the project manager responsible for the success of the project. Or, if one department is viewed as having a dominant role in the project, then a manager from that department (maybe the information systems department) may be assigned as the project manager.

The shortcomings of performing projects in functional organizations are:

- Weak project manager
- No direct funding
- Team members are more loyal to their departments than the project
- The rewards for completing the project are vague

The main goal of the manufacturing company is to manufacture widgets, for example, not to develop inventory systems. Such inventory projects lie outside the main goals of the organization, so the projects suffer because the organization does not have an efficient structure (at least for this project). On the other hand, the functional structure is flexible, requires no significant organizational changes, and can work well when the projects are not too big.

Matrix Organizations

The matrix organizational form merges the functional and dedicated project organizational forms to combine their advantages and overcome their disadvantages. Figure 6.1 shows a typical structure that characterizes the matrix form.

Figure 6.1 Matrix Organization

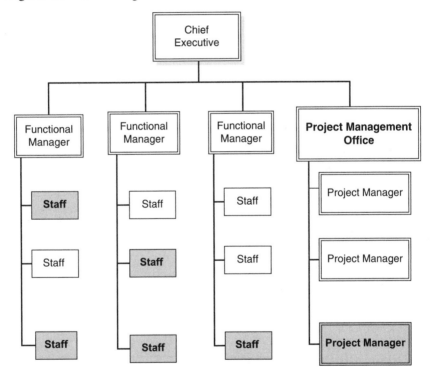

On the right, we see the project part of the organization. The project managers are often grouped into a program management office (PMO), which centralizes and coordinates the management of projects. PMOs may provide support functions such as training, standardized policies and tools, and archives of information.

The project manager builds a staff from the functional departments to accomplish the work of the project. This is indicated in the figure by the shaded boxes. Staff continue to report to their functional manager for all administrative purposes, in particular for their evaluation and rewards. However, for their work on the project, the staff report to the project manager. This is a distinctive characteristic of matrix management—people have "two bosses"—and this can be a source of great stress.

The project manager is responsible for schedules and milestones and decides what has to be done. The functional manager typically controls the technical performance of the project, i.e., how the job will be completed. The project manager negotiates with the functional manager about staff assignments and whether the activities have been completed satisfactorily.

One of the greatest benefits of using a matrix organization is that responsibility is shared between project and functional managers. Both maintain some degree of authority, responsibility, and accountability for the project. Use of a matrix organizational form is more collaborative than the functional and projectized forms. One of the greatest disadvantages of using a matrix organization is exactly the same as its strength. That is, responsibility is shared between project and functional managers.

Matrix management is a complex arrangement, and since each company is different, no two organizations will have the same matrix design. The strengths and weaknesses of matrix management are summarized in table 6.1.

Generally, in a matrix organization the project manager controls what the project team does and when they do it, while the functional manager controls who is assigned to the project and what technology is used.

Strong, Balanced, and Weak Matrix Organizations

There are various degrees of a matrix organization, referred to as strong, balanced, and weak.

> The words *strong* and *weak* refer to the power of the
> project manager.

Table 6.1 Project Issues in Matrix Organizations

Advantages	Disadvantages
Strong project focus	All decisions are negotiated between project and functional managers
Responsibility is shared between the project manager and functional managers	Staff report to two managers—project and functional
Project manager has access to entire company's resources	Team members may be shared
Flexible	Slow
Allows for participation on multiple projects	Stressful
Tasks can be performed in different locations	No dedicated project space
Consistent policies and procedures across many projects	Functional department goals are different from project goals
Efficient post-project transition	Staff must satisfy multiple bosses

A strong matrix is similar to a projectized organization. However, instead of the project being a stand-alone entity as it would be within a projectized organization, a strong matrix organization does not separate the project from the parent organization. In a strong matrix, the project manager has direct authority over resources assigned to the project.

A weak matrix is similar to a pure functional organization. When a company uses a weak matrix form, the project manager may be the only full-time team member, and the functional departments generally supply services to the project. In a weak matrix, the functional manager retains authority over resources.

A balanced matrix is the form indicated in figure 6.1. The project manager is responsible for the performance of the project, the schedule, and milestones. The functional manager assigns personnel from his or her department and is responsible for the technical performance of the work.

One of the characteristics of the balanced matrix form is that everything is negotiated. While the project manager is responsible for the schedule and milestones, these cannot be accomplished without taking into account the technical performance of the staff, which is the responsibility of the functional manager.

PROJECT STAFF

Projects require resources, which come in three categories: staff, equipment, and materials. Staff refers to the human resources and their skills and availability. Equipment consists of all of the special needs of the project, such as color printers or bulldozers. Materials covers all the remaining items needed by the project, such as blueprints, permits, and data in databases.

The availability of resources may seriously constrain the project's schedule. Equipment or personnel may only be available at specific times. Delays in the delivery of materials can seriously jeopardize a project's success.

The skills required by the various personnel and when they will be needed on the project are described in the staffing management plan. Hiring decisions are critical, and the project manager must work diligently at recruiting and retaining staff. What complicates the life of a project manager is that the assigned staff will most likely report to the functional manager. A project manager should understand the basic issues that affect how the project team is staffed, such as:

- Determining what personnel the project requires. This includes which skills are required and when, and then how many personnel are needed for each job category.
- Deciding whether the team members will come from within the organization or from outside sources
- Acknowledging the project organizational structure. Matrix organizational employees are still responsible to their functional managers, while in a projectized structure, team members will report to the project manager.

- Adjusting to the many staffing roles. Core team members are typically involved in a project from start to finish. These individuals usually include the project manager and any team members who have critical or unique knowledge. Other team members may be involved only for the time it takes them to complete specific tasks.

- Managing the many supporting roles. Many departments play a supporting role, such as legal, accounting, training, environmental, marketing, publishing, and safety.

Staffing options include using people from within your own department, people from other departments in the organization, subcontractors, consultants, and external vendors. Each option has pros and cons, and the project manager has to determine which alternative is most appropriate, based on the associated costs and schedules.

A few things about staffing should be noted:

- Staffing constraints can affect the network diagram. Adding people can shorten the duration of an activity. However, it is also possible that staff are only available at specific times or maybe in a certain order.

- The network diagram usually results in a staff loading that has lots of peaks and valleys in it. It is difficult to put people onto a project and then remove them soon afterward, only to ask them back again after a short time. The project manager should attempt to level the staff loading so it is more reasonable. This is called resource leveling. Such leveling also applies to things like equipment.

- The resource allocation problem gets very complicated, very fast. There are no easy rules to use. The only real way to manage the resources is for the project manager to understand the details of the project. The project manager can then propose staff movements and activity assignments, and determine their impact.

Although the problem is difficult, there are a few simple things to examine:

- Start with our old friend the critical path.

- Look for activities with slack and move staff off them to other activities (this delays noncritical activities).

- Try to complete activities in parallel.

- Use the priority matrix to help decide which activities to delay, or which requirements to downgrade, or how much cost to incur (the triple constraint).

MONITORING AND CONTROLLING PROJECTS

One of the most complex parts of project management is the monitoring and controlling of projects. There are massive amounts of information to consider on dozens of topics. Table 6.2 shows the monitoring and controlling process group, which contains the following processes:

Table 6.2 Monitoring and Controlling Process Group

• Monitor and control project work—collecting, measuring, and disseminating information	• Perform quality control—monitoring results for conformance to standards
• Integrated change control—ensuring that changes are beneficial	• Manage project team—tracking team member performance
• Scope verification—accepting completed deliverables	• Performance reporting—collecting and distributing performance information
• Scope control—controlling changes to the scope	• Manage stakeholders—managing communications and resolving issues
• Schedule control—controlling changes to the schedule	• Risk monitoring and control—tracking, identifying, and evaluating risks
• Cost control—controlling changes to the budget	• Contract administration—managing contractual relationships

With so many issues to worry about, how does a project manager cope? By focusing on three essential concepts:

- The critical path
- Integrated change control
- Accurately measuring the progress of deliverables

As the project proceeds, many different types of changes are proposed and must be evaluated: new features are proposed, cost and schedule slippages occur, risks emerge, team members join and leave. Constantly monitoring the above three concepts allows the project manager to stay in control. As changes flood in, the project manager must first assess the impact of each one on the critical path. Proposed new features are objectively evaluated to determine their relative usefulness versus cost and schedule impact. The project manager must evaluate each change for its impact on the critical path, because changes there immediately impact the cost and schedule.

Next, the change control process is followed so that proposed changes are communicated to all stakeholders, who then have a chance to express their views.

Finally, the status of the project is continually measured. The key to evaluating accurately the true progress of a project is to measure the status of all deliverables. Only by focusing on deliverables can the actual progress be measured. Deliverables are tangible entities—you know them when you see them. In chapter 12, we will delve into this in detail. For now, we summarize the process by noting that only when a deliverable is complete can you assess its worth. Assuming the deliverables have the requisite quality, that is they meet their specified performance requirements, the status of the project can be accurately assessed.

The Importance of the Critical Path

An amazing statistic, quoted in the textbook by Clifford Gray and Erik Larson, is that only ten percent of the activities in a project are on the critical path. This makes the project manager's life much easier. Consider this: If all activities are equally likely to go wrong, then there is only a ten percent chance that this will result in a problem for the project.

When any issue arises, the project manger should immediately consult the critical path and ask the question, "What is the impact of this issue on the CP?" The answer to this question will immediately tell you the priority of the issue. Of course, one must be sensitive to the fact that accumulating issues in noncritical activities can quickly add up to a critical problem, and then require urgent attention.

Here is a list of practical actions a project manager can perform to improve the chance of success:

- Assign the best people to critical activities.
- Prioritize discussions about critical activities.
- Perform risk assessment on critical activities first.
- Regularly visit people working on critical activities.
- Assign overtime to people working on critical activities.
- Assign the best technology and tools to critical activities.
- Examine schedule changes to determine their impact on the critical path.

One can also "roll up" noncritical activities. That is, one can take a large number of activities in the network diagram and treat them as a single entity. This reduces the complexity of presentations about the project.

Integrated Change Control

Because changes are a normal part of a project, integrated change control is practiced throughout the life of the project. The details change with the size and complexity of the project, but the essential features are the following:

- Identifying all changes and their rationale and documenting their impact
- Controlling the scope, cost, budget, and schedule by coordinating changes
- Maintaining the integrity of baselines by regulating the flow of changes and only allowing approved changes to be implemented
- Constantly reviewing approved changes and validating defect repair

A formal configuration management system establishes the method through which changes are identified, implemented, and controlled. It also provides a method for the communication of changes to all stakeholders. All proposed changes must follow the steps in the change control system to assure that only formally accepted proposals are implemented.

SCHEDULE COMPRESSION TECHNIQUES

There are two important techniques used to compress a project schedule. Both of them assume that the project scope does not change. While the details can be complex, the concepts involved are quite straightforward.

Crashing is a schedule compression technique in which cost and schedule trade-offs are analyzed to determine the costs associated with reductions in the project duration. One example of crashing is to propose adding more staff to a critical path activity to shorten its schedule. Adding people will usually increase the cost. Also, it won't usually cause a linear compression in schedule. For example, doubling the number of people on an activity will not necessarily result in halving the time because of the increased communication between the staff members. Crashing compresses the schedule, but usually at increased cost, and it does not always produce a viable plan.

Fast-tracking is another schedule compression technique. Here, tasks that are supposed to be performed in sequence are redesigned to be performed in parallel. For example, it is normal to begin construction only after the design is completed and its quality is reviewed. However, you may propose to start construction when design is 75 percent complete. While this might compress the schedule, it certainly adds risks to the project. If the design is revised during the quality review cycle, completed construction activities may need to be reworked. Fast-tracking compresses the schedule, but increases the risks.

MONITORING AND CONTROLLING IN ACTION: BOSTON'S BIG DIG

The Central Artery/Tunnel Project, replacing Boston's inner-city infrastructure with new roads, bridges, and tunnels, proved to be one of the largest, most technically difficult and environmentally challenging infrastructure projects ever undertaken in the United States. Known informally as the

"Big Dig," the project spanned 7.8 miles of highway, about half in tunnels. The larger of the two Charles River bridges, a ten-lane cable-stayed hybrid bridge, is the widest bridge ever built and the first to use an asymmetrical design. The Big Dig was a public work on a scale comparable to some of the great projects of the last century—the Panama Canal, the English Channel Tunnel (the "Chunnel"), and the Trans-Alaska Pipeline.

Every monitoring and control technique that could be conceived of was used and applied to the Big Dig, and the studies, their results, and the data are all available to the public. There was no shortage of monitoring on the Big Dig. One might argue, however, that there was an acute shortage of control.

When the Central Artery/Tunnel Project was first conceived in 1983 to alleviate traffic gridlock in Boston, the cost was estimated at $2.56 billion. Costs and schedules were updated annually, and the cost gradually increased to $7.74 billion in 1992, to $10.4 billion in 1994, and the most recent estimate of $14.79 billion in 2008. See figure 6.2.

The Big Dig placed 3.8 million cubic yards of concrete—the equivalent of 2,350 acres—one foot thick. The Big Dig also excavated more than 16 million cubic yards of soil. Monitoring of the progress, therefore, could always be measured in terms of the concrete poured and the soil excavated. In fact, the contractor, Bechtel/Parsons Brinckerhoff, claims that their estimate of $14 billion was reached as far back as 1992. Meanwhile, as late as 2000, public officials were still announcing "revised estimates" of $12.2 billion.

Figure 6.3 Cost Growth Categories on the "Big Dig."

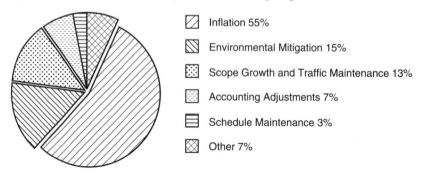

☑ Inflation 55%

◪ Environmental Mitigation 15%

▦ Scope Growth and Traffic Maintenance 13%

▢ Accounting Adjustments 7%

▤ Schedule Maintenance 3%

▨ Other 7%

"Other" category includes differing site conditions, quantity variations, design development, pricing variations, cost containment credits, and contingency.

Cost control at the Big Dig relied on traditional project management methods: a work breakdown schedule with resources assigned. Each contract was divided into specific tasks with required resources and scheduled milestones. As contract modifications were proposed and implemented, additional activities were added to the schedule and the work breakdown structure.

Schedule control was maintained by monitoring work in progress. Contractors developed detailed schedules for their own work that were aggregated into the overall project schedule. Scheduling was implemented using a commercial software package, Primavera™, which was in widespread use in the construction industry.

Senior project management reviewed significant scope changes as part of the contract modification process. Big Dig monthly reports included milestone dates and contingency dates, but they did not necessarily offer realistic completion dates, and this created problems with public credibility. In fact, the constant revisions of costs and schedules dramatically reduced the public's confidence in Big Dig management.

TEST YOURSELF

1. Profit Calculation

   Your project is planned to cost $100,000 and take 12 months to complete. The customer has agreed to a fee of $10,000. The customer would like you to finish the project early and so has proposed an early completion incentive fee. The reward for an early finish is $5,000 per month, and that is to be split 50/50 between you and the customer. If the project is late, there is a penalty clause, and you will pay $10,000 per month.

   a. If the project finishes one month early, what is your fee percentage?

   b. If the project finishes one month late, what is your fee percentage?

2. Critical Path Issue

   You are taking your wife to Madrid for your anniversary. You have planned the trip and part of the critical path consists of the following activities: drive home from work, pack, load car with luggage, and drive to airport. Make a backup plan to allow for the fact that you may get held up at work. How does this affect the critical path?

Tip: Give your answer in project management language.

KEY POINTS TO REMEMBER

- Managing stakeholder expectations reduces conflict over competing requirements and establishes unambiguous acceptance criteria for project deliverables.

- Projects in matrix organizations are complicated by negotiations between project and functional managers.

- The project manager manages by focusing on three essential concepts:

  - The critical path

  - Integrated change control

  - Accurately measuring the progress of deliverables

- When any changes are proposed, first examine the impact on the critical path.

- Always follow the integrated change control process so that stakeholders understand the impact of changes and only approved changes are implemented.

- Project status can only be accurately measured in terms of completed deliverables.

- Any one change to performance, cost, or schedule will affect the entire performance, cost, and schedule.

- Crashing compresses the schedule, but increases the cost. Fast-tracking compresses the schedule, but increases the risks.

Closing and Contracts

INTRODUCTION

The focus of this activity is on formal acceptance and approval of the project deliverables by the sponsors and documenting lessons learned.

Closing a project involves formally terminating all activities associated with a project. If the project has been successfully completed, then this involves verifying that all contractual obligations have been satisfied. Even if the project was cancelled before completion, many of the same activities must be completed. Lessons learned for unsuccessful projects may be even more valuable.

WHAT'S AHEAD

- The details of closing a project
- Contract types
  - Fixed price contracts
  - Cost plus contracts
  - Time and material contracts
- Contract changes
- Risks associated with fixed price, cost plus, and time and material contracts

IN THE REAL WORLD

The salespeople were promised an upgrade for their laptops to the new Vista operating system. Many of them were on sales calls and traveling on extended trips. The technical people were waiting to upgrade the software according to the project plan.

The salespeople showed up after their trips, expecting to get the upgrade. The technical people said, "You're too late! We have started another project."

The project manager had to use all her negotiation skills to induce the salespeople and the technical people to agree to a new schedule for the upgrades. The project cannot be closed out until everyone is satisfied, which in this case involves chasing down all of the salespeople and finding a time when the technical people can upgrade their laptops. Only when all of the units are converted will the project be complete. Payment will only occur when all these details are finally completed and documented.

KEY CONCEPTS

CONTRACT CLOSEOUT

Closing is a real challenge and takes a long time. There are a myriad of complicated details, both technical and financial, that must be taken care of. Failure to correctly deal with any of the details will hold up contract closure.

Contract closure is the one of the processes in the closing process group. Closure involves ensuring that all contract work has been completed and accepted, performing an audit to ensure that all deliverables are of acceptable quality (i.e., they meet their specified requirements), and creating an archive for the contract documentation.

If the project has been determined to be unsuccessful and is prematurely terminated, then contract closure might be a mutual agreement between the customer and the project team to terminate the project.

Contract closure can even result from a default of one of the parties. In either case, the termination clause in the contract will determine the rights and responsibilities of each party.

Contract closeout usually includes the following:

- Stakeholder debriefings
- Documentation of contract closure
- Procurement audits
- Handing off of deliverables
- Final acceptance and payment

An important part of contract closure that is gaining more importance is the completion of lessons learned. The lessons, both good and bad, along with process improvements and recommendations, are archived. Future project managers may search and examine the database both as a learning tool and for ideas and approaches.

Such information will come in handy should the organization become involved in another project similar in nature. You then have a sample of the WBS and risks in the project plan. The project manager also uses this as an opportunity to provide feedback on staff performance on the project.

A final project report is also created and published. The content of such a report is indicated in table 7.1.

Projects may also terminate for reasons besides completion of the deliverables. For example:

- A merger between companies may require consolidation of projects.
- The product may become technically obsolete before the project is complete.
- The business case for the project may become obsolete before the project is complete.
- Poor performance may result in cancellation of the project, either due to lateness and cost overruns, or poor product quality.

Table 7.1 Project Closure Report

Client Name
Project Background and Description
Summary of Project Results
Reason for Closing the Project
Deliverables Evaluation
Project Schedule: Original and Actual Start and End Dates
Project Team
Outstanding Risks
Budget and Financial Information: Original and Actual
Action Plan
Ongoing Support
Next Steps or Transition Plan
Project Closure Approval
Appendix A
Project Management–Related Documentation
Appendix B
Product-Related Documentation

Lack of proper closure can result in frustration. The project manager should acknowledge the contributions of the team and stakeholders, preferably in a tangible manner. Just as the charter kicks off the project with enthusiasm, closing a project should be a cause for celebration. This should be seen as an opportunity to market the project's accomplishments and successes.

Lessons Learned

History might repeat itself unless your learn from your mistakes. At the end of the project, the team should complete a table such as the one that follows and file it in the company archives. Before the start of a similar project, any or all such lessons should be reviewed.

Table 7.2 Lessons learned from Vista Project

Phase	What Worked?	What did not work?	Lessons for next Project
Initiation	Team building: Identified a good mix of team members	Not enough effort in defining the scope.	Spend more time identifying the scope: which users are local, which are remote
Planning	Clear WBS identified activities and this resulted in a good network diagram.	Team members struggled to identify a good communications strategy	Use a single repository for all information.
Execution	The schedule and activity assignments were clearly communicated to everyone.	Users were not releasing the computers on time for upgrades.	Distribute information to remote users earlier and more closely monitor their travel schedule.
Monitoring and Controlling	Having visible milestones and prioritizing completion of critical path items.	Earned value analysis was not done and activity costs and schedules were uncertain.	Invest in earned value training and tools.
Closing Phase	Survey of users was conducted—and yielded valuable insight.	The remote user's laptops were upgraded late and contractors were not paid on time.	Coordinate with controller's office for partial payment based on percent work completed.

Table 7.3 Procurement Management

• Plan purchases and acquisitions—determining what to purchase, the means, and when	• Request seller responses—reviewing offers and negotiating contracts
• Plan contracting—documenting products and services and identifying potential sellers	• Contract administration—managing the contract with the customer and any sellers
	• Contract closure—completing and settling each contract

PROCUREMENT MANAGEMENT

Procurement management includes the acquistion process for any products or services needed for the project from outside the company. Procurement management consists of the processes shown in table 7.3.

A contract is a legal document between a buyer and seller. It is a mutually binding agreement that obligates the seller to provide specified products and services, and it also obligates the buyer to provide monetary or other valuable consideration. For a project, the contract will typically contain the scope document, which then becomes the definition of what the project must do. Most organizations have very detailed policies and procedures that specify precisely who can sign a contract and make legally binding commitments.

The project manager helps to define the contract to reflect the specific needs of the project. One of the most important features of a contract is the process by which changes to it are accomplished. The legally binding nature of a contract means that the change and approval processes are reviewed thoroughly by company management.

A contract typically contains a "Terms and Conditions" clause, which may specify major deliverables, key milestones, and costs. This clause may also require customer approval of major staffing roles. The contract may also include references to "Technical Requirements," such as environmental regulations, government standards, health regulations, local and state ordinances, etc.

TYPES OF CONTRACTS

Contracts fall into the following general categories:
- Fixed price
- Cost plus
- Time and material

There is considerable variation within each category, but the key difference between the contract types is the assumption of risk. Who assumes the risk for each type of contract and what are the implications?

Fixed Price (FP) Contracts

This type of contract involves the delivery of a well-defined product for a fixed price. A fixed price contract may include incentives for meeting or exceeding specified objectives, including cost and schedule targets.

A very simple form of fixed price contract is a purchase order for an item to be delivered on a specified date for a specified price. This demonstrates the attractive simplicity of fixed price contracts. When there is a well-defined product, it can be acquired with a fixed price contract.

For most projects, however, constant change is a fact of life, and it is difficult to precisely define the end product. This puts a huge burden on the preparer of the contract because it is difficult and costly to develop a complete specification. But for fixed price contracts, development of the specification is critical.

In fixed price contracts, negotiations about adjustments and changes can be contentious. The contractor is in a good position if changes are required, because it is unlikely that another company can do the job. To combat this, a fixed price contract may include incentives for the contractor to complete the job earlier and for less cost. This helps to mitigate the risk of the contractor asking for more money, since the additional funds may come at the expense of the incentives.

The following table explains the risks for a fixed price contract.

Table 7.4 Risks in a Fixed Price Contract

Customer Risks	Contractor Risks
• Contract is expensive because development of the specification is time-consuming • Incomplete specification leads to contract changes • At the mercy of a sole source contractor for add-ons • Tendency of the contractor to use cheaper materials	• Requires careful estimation of the cost • Requires careful estimation of the schedule • Growth in costs can lead to unprofitable projects

Cost Plus Contracts

In this type of contract, the seller is paid for the actual costs incurred plus a fee representing the seller's profit. Costs are classified as direct and indirect. Direct costs are those applicable directly to the project. They are usually dominated by the project salaries, but also include equipment and travel. Indirect costs are usually allocated as a percentage of direct costs and cover occupancy expenses (rent, heat, electric, etc.), benefits (vacations and sick pay), and company administrative costs (payroll, etc.).

The most common types of cost plus contracts are cost plus fixed fee (CPFF) and cost plus incentive fee (CPIF).

Cost Plus Fixed Fee (CPFF)

In a CPFF contract, the seller is reimbursed for all allowable costs (both direct and indirect) incurred while performing on the project. The seller typically reports all of the direct costs to the customer. The indirect costs are usually calculated and negotiated as a percentage.

In a CPFF contract, the fee is fixed, no matter what the cost. The contract may initially estimate the cost of the project as $100,000 with a 6 percent fee (fee = $6,000, for a total project cost of $106,000). The actual project costs may rise to $200,000, but the contractor still only receives a fixed fee of $6,000.

When it is very difficult to define the end product, a CPFF contract is appropriate. This reduces the burden on the customer to prepare a complete specification. The customer assumes more of the cost risk. While the contractor is reimbursed for all actual costs, as costs rise the fee percentage declines.

For CPFF contracts, the contractor is again in a good position if changes are required, because it is unlikely that another company can do the job. To combat the tendency of the contractor to just keep adding costs, there are usually negotiated cost control procedures that must be followed. These are typically tied to the project's change control process so that add-ons are clearly justified.

The following table explains the risks for a CPFF contract.

Table 7.5 Risks in a CPFF Contract

Customer Risks	Contractor Risks
• Poor specification leads to more costs	• Fee percentage declines as costs rise
• Relying on the goodwill of the contractor to control costs	• Rising costs may damage the relationship with the customer
• Incomplete specification leads to contract changes	
• At the mercy of a sole source contractor for add-ons	
• Final cost unknown	

Cost Plus Incentive Fee (CPIF)

A CPIF contract is very similar to a CPFF contract. The seller is again reimbursed for all allowable costs (both direct and indirect) and receives a predetermined fee. However, the fee may change depending on the contract incentives. The contractor may be rewarded with extra payments for completing the job ahead of schedule or for less than the estimated cost.

The contractor may also be penalized for delivering poor quality or completing the project late (disincentives). In some contracts, if the final costs are less than the estimate, both the buyer and the seller may share the savings.

The risks and rewards of a CPIF contract are very similar to those of a CPFF contract. The disadvantage of the CPFF contract is that the seller has little incentive to lower costs. The rationale for the CPIF contract is to give the contractor reasons to complete the project in a way that is favorable to the customer.

Time and Materials (T&M) Contracts

This type of contract contains features of both fixed fee and cost plus contracts. In a T&M contract, the customer is buying the services of a contractor and agrees to pay for the number of hours worked at a defined rate. Like a cost plus contract, a T&M contract is open-ended and thus can grow. However, T&M contracts resemble fixed price contracts in that the rates for service are fixed at the time of the contract.

Table 7.6 Risks in a T&M Contract

Customer Risks	Contractor Risks
• No specification	• Fixed rates
• Open-ended	• No defined tasks
• At the mercy of a sole source contractor for add-ons	

Figure 7.1 Relation Between Scope, Risk, and Contract Type

Scope	Very Little	Little	Partial	Fairly Complete	Complete
Uncertainty/ Risk	High		Medium		Low
Contract Types	Cost +%	Cost +% + Incentive	Cost + Fixed Fee	Fixed Price + Incentive	Firm Fixed Price
Risk Allocation	Contractor Risk 0%				Seller Risk 100%

Figure 7.1 summarizes the relation between scope, risk, and contract types. If the scope is complete, then a fixed price contract is appropriate, and the contractor bears 100 percent of the risk. On the other hand, if very little is known about the scope of the project, the risk and uncertainty is very high, and a cost plus contract is appropriate.

If the scope information is partially known, then a cost plus contract with incentives may be appropriate. Typically, cost incentives may be for finishing early or completing the job below some target price.

CONTRACT CHANGES

In any contract, one of the most important considerations is the Contract Change Control System (CCS). The CCS defines the process by which a contract's authorized scope may be modified.

The customer must watch out for the tendency of the contractor to take advantage of the customer by proposing changes. If a deficiency in a product is found during development, the customer has several options:

- Change the specification to agree with the product as is.
- Change the specification and pay for an upgrade.
- Change the testing criteria so the product passes the test.
- Change the training manual so the users know how to use the product as is.
- Insist that the contractor pay for the fix.

All of these options will be reasonable solutions to different sorts of problems. Therefore, change control negotiations can get very complicated. For each of the proposed solutions, the customer and the project manager have different goals and objectives.

CLOSURE IN ACTION

You are about to move into your new house. The moving van is pulling up to your old house. Before loading the moving van, you decide to go over to the new house for a quick look around. When you get there, the builder refuses to let you in.

The builder is standing there holding the keys, but waiting for a piece of paper from the bank. The financial transaction was held up by a technical glitch. Even though the funds left your account yesterday, the contract is not complete.

These types of issues are common challenges in project closure. The project manager should allow for unknowns and should have developed contingencies.

TEST YOURSELF

What contract types are appropriate for the following scenarios?

1. A pharmaceutical company is developing a cure for migraine headaches from an herb discovered in South America. The company subcontracts out the testing of the drug on human subjects

2. Building a two-car garage

3. Building a road

4. Conducting a campaign for charity

5. What are the steps involved in closing the 50th anniversary project? (Hint: What items would be on the checklist?)

KEY POINTS TO REMEMBER

- Closing a project involves terminating all activities associated with a project.
- Closure involves:
  - Ensuring that all contract work has been completed and accepted
  - Performing an audit to ensure that all deliverables are of acceptable quality
  - Creating an archive for the contract documentation
  - Adding the lessons learned to the company archive
- Contracts fall into the following general categories:
  - Fixed price, when the scope is well known
  - Cost plus, when the scope is poorly known
  - Time and materials, an open-ended contract for small projects which is used when the scope is not defined

Project Communications

Up to 90 percent of a project manager's time is spent in communications.
—Project Management Institute (PMI)

INTRODUCTION

Communications is about making everyone aware of what is going on in the project at all times. Managing project communications is one of the most important duties of a project manager. Project managers must inform sponsors, team members, management, and others about project status, while constantly evaluating where the project is and where it is going.

WHAT'S AHEAD

- Key project communication processes
- Identifying and communicating with stakeholders
- Communications planning
- Distribution of communications
- Performance reporting
- Relation to the PMBOK
- Test yourself
- Key points to remember

IN THE REAL WORLD

Jim Cormier, his wife, and two small children were in a hotel room when the fire alarm sounded. His wife was the first to be awakened by the alarm, and her perception of the message was clear and loud: "Danger! For safety's sake, evacuate the hotel."

She shook Jim awake until he heard the alarm, and she was very surprised by his complacent reaction. Jim had just finished a project which involved moving into a new building. One of the problems he had encountered in this new building was a fire alarm system that sounded randomly throughout the day. All the employees had to evacuate the building. There was never a fire, and Jim had experienced many unnecessary evacuations. With this experience, his perception of the message was the ambiguous, "Possible danger—possible system malfunction."

This real-world story clearly indicates the complexity of communications in the real world. A simple message, loud and clear, is interpreted by two relatively similar receivers in different ways. Project management always involves multiple team members and multiple stakeholders, all of whom have different perspectives. This constantly creates challenges in communication.

A large body of research clearly suggests that project communications management is a huge challenge in almost all projects. A project manager with strong communication skills can help a team overcome serious communication problems.

KEY CONCEPTS

What are examples of project communications? We have already seen references to the following project communications: project charters, project plans, status reports, and earned value reports. Communication activities involve developing a communications management plan, managing stakeholders, distributing project information in a timely manner, motivating teams, and resolving conflicts. The project manager must also determine what type of information should be communicated, including the level of detail and with what frequency.

COMMUNICATION THEORY

The following key points stem from management literature. They are not unique to project management, so we do not go into them in detail here. Regardless, it is important for us to present the following core issues involved with project human resource management and communications.

Communications Model

All communications models involve the following: a sender, recipient, message, and medium. The sender is the person sending the message to the receiver. The receiver is the recipient of the message. Messages are encoded and decoded using a device or technology before they travel over the medium. The medium is the path of the message, such as email or phone. The parties involved in communications must confirm that they understand the message being sent. This process involves listening, using techniques such as feedback, active listening, or interpreting nonverbal communication such as hand gestures and body language. Nonverbal communication can account for more than 50 percent of typical communication.

Filters

There are filters on both the sender's and receiver's sides that hinder communication; examples of filters are listed below:

- Language, technical material, lack of clear communication channels, physical separation, personality conflicts, culture, semantics, and message content (could be intertwined with hidden agendas)
- Environmental background: psychological and sociological parameters, dysfunctional emotional behaviors, different educational backgrounds
- Authority/reputation
- Predetermined mind-set; having a self-fulfilling philosophy or unfounded assumptions
- Historical consideration: the way a task was always done

Barriers

Finally, there are communication barriers in communications models, including mumbling, long distance, static, and negative attitudes. More examples are listed below:

- Noise
- Preoccupation
- Power games
- Withholding of information
- Management by memo
- Hostility
- Filters (see the list above)

COMMUNICATION CHANNELS

Communication can become a very complex activity in large project settings. Following is a simple formula that will calculate the lines of communication or the communication channels based on the number of people involved in a project.

$$\text{Lines of communication} = N\,(N-1)/2$$

For example, if you have four people communicating, you will have six lines of communication:

$$\text{Lines of Communication} = 4(4-1)/2 = 6$$

But if you add an additional person to your team, this now means that N is equal to five people, and therefore there are ten lines of communication.

Notice that the communication complexity has almost doubled by adding just one more person to the team. This is the reason that project managers divide complex activities down to three-people teams so that the lines of communication are limited. With three people in a team cluster, there are only three lines of communication.

KEY PROJECT COMMUNICATION PROCESSES

The primary goal of project communications is to share information with all stakeholders: team members, project sponsors, vendors, and other parties affected by the project. Following the project communication processes will ensure that communication occurs and that it occurs when needed. A good framework for project communications is presented in the PMBOK standard. There are four processes associated with project communications (see Figure 8.1):

1. Communication planning: Determining information and communication needs for the project

2. Information distribution: Making needed information available to project stakeholders in a timely manner, as well as responding to unexpected requests for information

3. Performance reporting: Collecting and distributing performance information—includes status reporting, progress measurement, and forecasting

4. Managing stakeholders

The communication management plan is the primary output of the communications planning process. This plan is created by the project manager and becomes part of the project plan. The purpose is to inform all stakeholders how and in what form communications will be handled on the project.

The communications plan answers fundamental questions pertaining to the project, such as the following: What information needs to be communicated? Who will communicate this information and subsequently make decisions? How will other pertinent information be distributed and in what format? How will schedules and other reports be distributed throughout the project? What communication will take place and with whom, in case there is a variance?

Figure 8.1 Communications Processes

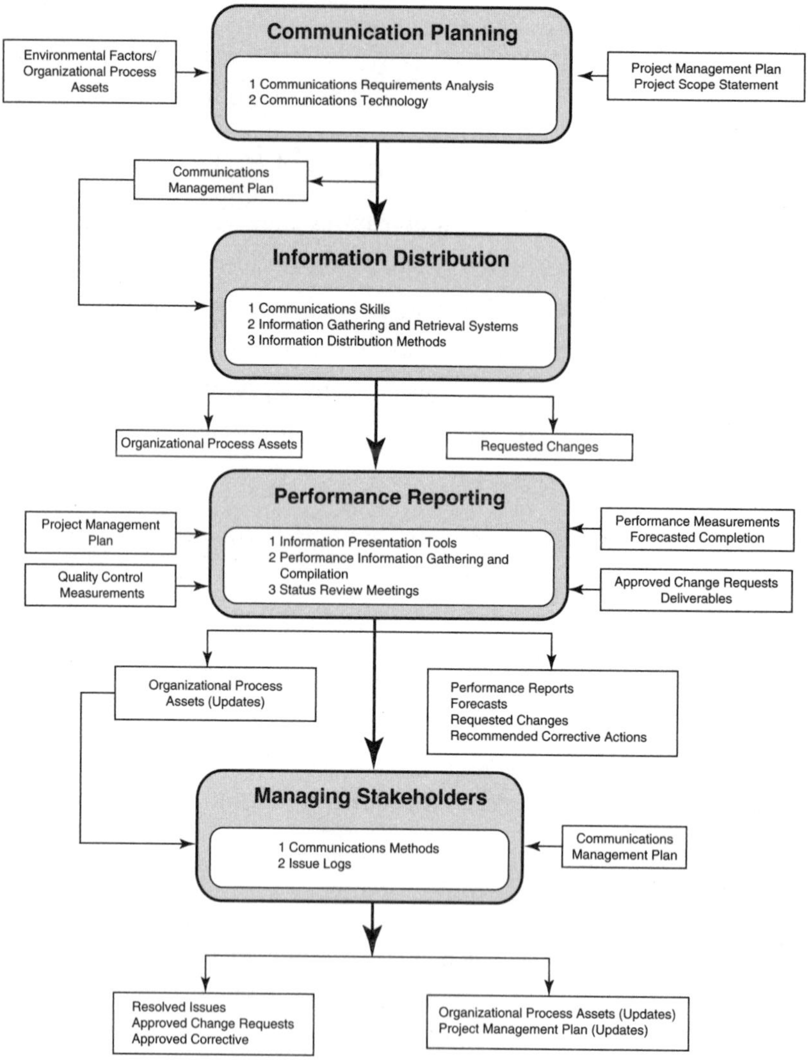

The other key outputs of project communications are organizational process assets, performance reports, forecasts, earned value reports, issues, change requests, and corrective actions. The key components of a communication plan are illustrated in table 8.1.

Here you should list any rules, either company or regulatory, that exist at your company, the client company, or the vendor's company on what things and how things can be communicated.

Table 8.1 Communication Plan

1.	Introduction			
2.	List steering committee and all stakeholder groups, with a description of the purpose of the group and a list of all members for each group.			
3.	Formal Communication Schedule/Plan			
	Communication	Content	Objective	Owner
	Audience	Method	Frequency/ Date	
4.	Communication	Recipients	Method	Timing
	(What)	(Whom)	(How)	(When)
5.	Communication Rules			

IDENTIFYING AND COMMUNICATING WITH STAKEHOLDERS

Identifying and communicating with stakeholders is important. Projects bring value to their stakeholders. The success of a project can therefore be influenced by stakeholders. The project manager may have to manage stakeholders who were not communicated with during the project initiation phase. They may set up roadblocks for the project manager throughout the project.

To ensure sound decision-making throughout the project's life, you must identify stakeholders early. Stakeholders can be found within the sponsoring organization and outside. Consider this quote in the *New York Times*:

Hydro-Quebec is now in the center of a storm over a proposed project that would spend 12.6 billion Canadian dollars to tap hydropower on the Great Whale River, which flows into Hudson Bay. The project is intensely opposed by the Cree Indians who live in the area and by environmentalists. The dispute has spread to the United States, where opponents are pressing New York and Vermont to restrain purchases of power from Quebec even as growth in power demand is slowing. New York, which currently gets only a tiny percentage of its power from Quebec, has delayed until late next year a final decision on proceeding with a contract to pay 14.5 billion American dollars over 21 years for power from Quebec.

Hydro-Quebec has invested millions of dollars in this project, but did not successfully identify or influence stakeholders. They underestimated the impact of various project stakeholders and did not consider stakeholders outside the immediate project boundaries.

Some of the stakeholder categories in this case are listed in table 8.2.

Table 8.2 Stakeholder Categories

Internal	External
Project team members	Impacted users
Funding authority	Regulatory bodies
Finance	Environmentalists
Quality assurance	Standard certification agencies
Legal	Government agencies
Users	Users of related products
Executives	Venture capitalists

It might not be possible to satisfy the constraints of all key stakeholders at the same time. It is a fact that in most large projects, stakeholders have interests at odds with each other. Therefore, it is important to rank the stakeholders by influence and also to conduct a brief stakeholder analysis. For example:

Stakeholder:	Environmental Protection Agency
Value:	Preventing harm and danger to the citizen
Influence:	High
Win condition:	Proper testing conducted

Stakeholder:	Environmentalists
Value:	Enhance environmental benefits or prevent damage to environment
Influence:	Medium to high
Win condition:	Consideration of their views

One should focus on negotiating achievable commitments with stakeholders and reaching a consensus with stakeholders with conflicting interests. This is easy to do if the precise "win" condition for each stakeholder is identified. Finally, the nature of the project itself may change due to views of stakeholders, so it is important to do a stakeholder analysis before any detailed planning is done.

Once stakeholders are identified, the RACI method can be used to clearly identify the roles of the stakeholders. The acronym is explained below.

Responsible (R): Those who do work to achieve the task

Accountable (A): This could be the Approver. This resource is answerable for the correct completion of the task. There is only one "A" specified for each task.

Consulted (C): Those whose opinions are sought

Informed (I): Those who are kept up-to-date on progress

Table 8.3 The RACI Responsibilities

	Tong	**Bob**	**Eileen**
Project charter	R	R	A
Scope statement	R	A	I
WBS	A	R	I
Cost estimate	I	C	A
Procurement plan	R	A	I
Risk plan	A	C	R
HR plan	I	A	R

DISTRIBUTION METHODS

Let us talk briefly about the forms that communications will take and some of the methods for using them effectively. One can communicate verbally or in written form and one can do so informally or formally. So we have four methods associated with project communications: formal written, formal verbal, informal written, and informal verbal.

For example, team meetings are regarded as informal verbal. The delivery of a technical specification for review purposes can be regarded as a formal written document. Letters written to sponsors delineating status are also formal written communications.

Table 8.4 Communication Methods and Their Usage

Communication Method	When Used
Formal written	Complex problems, project plans, project charter
Formal verbal	Presentations, speeches
Informal written	Memos, emails, notes
Informal verbal	Meetings, conversations

Note that email is regarded as informal written. Project managers may use email to communicate things that are noncontroversial, nonthreatening, and nonpersonal. Email is not the right media for letting a team member know that they are not performing well or that they need to improve. The risks with email are misinterpretation of tone and intent. Even a simple meeting reminder to a stakeholder or sponsor might appear to be rude or demanding.

Another risk with email is the fact that even informal conversation about quality issues is permanently recorded, and now due to compliance regulations, such emails can be retrieved for investigation purposes. Additionally, emails add to the load of already full inboxes of the parties involved.

TEAMS

Stages in Team Formation

From the very outset, the project manager is involved with personnel from backgrounds with different amounts of expertise. The project manager has to get to know the team members very well in order to identify their roles and responsibilities and also set performance expectations. The project manager has to ensure that the team members have the needed skills and training early on in the life of the project. When the project manager composes the team, the following criteria can be used:

- Experience or skills match project requirements: business, leadership, and technical
- Personal desire or interest matches project goals
- Accessibility
- Availability
- Working style matches team style

Most new teams go through the following five stages of team formation:

1. Forming
   - During this stage, the team members get acquainted with each other for the first time.
   - They are motivated and excited about the project.
   - During the kickoff meeting, the project manager should leverage this opportunity to lay the ground rules for a sound foundation.

2. Storming
   - During this stage, differences in style and personality amongst team members surface.
   - Interpersonal behaviors and process issues create conflict.

- The project manager should be supportive at this stage and proactive in handling issues.

3. Norming
   - Team members start working together.
   - The project manager should ensure that there is full participation from all the members.

4. Performing
   - Team members work productively at this stage.
   - The project manager should motivate team members and provide resources.

5. Mourning
   - The project is at the closing phase.
   - Team members may be focusing on their next project.
   - The project manager should ease the transition for team members to the new project.
   - Project manager should ensure that lessons learned are documented.

Team Building

The focus of team building is training, feedback, reward, and recognition. The steps to be followed are:

- Determine skills requirements.
- Interview potential team members.
- Select team members.
- Hold a kickoff meeting.
- Clarify roles and expectations.
- Describe your management process.
- Establish a good basis for open communication.

One of the key responsibilities for the project manager is to provide opportunities for team members to provide valued input. Weekly team meetings provide the opportunity to enhance communications. Typically for such meetings, the project manager will set the agenda with the objective and goals for the meeting and will email compiled status reports before the meeting. The project manager will assign who will make decisions on approving tasks and choosing resources, will assign deliverables on a weekly or monthly basis, and will report on the project expectations from the management's viewpoint.

Techniques for conducting successful meetings are not any different from traditional meetings:

- Start the meeting at the scheduled time.
- Follow the agenda items that were emailed ahead of time.
- Ensure that all team members have an opportunity to report project status.
- Investigate existing and new risks/issues and assign action items.
- Determine the next steps or next meeting time.
- End on time.

A key point is to make sure that the project manager has given all team members an opportunity to give a status update and indicate if they see any new issues or risks. The project manager must keep everyone focused on the project and run effective meetings. The project manager must be a good listener—this is a key concern from team members. Surveys reveal the following team members' concerns about their project manager:

- Unreasonable expectations
- Doesn't show interest in me
- Doesn't have time for me
- Is inconsistent
- Doesn't recognize or show appreciation
- Seems disorganized
- Doesn't take care of the team
- Sets unreasonable expectations

From the Experience Vault

Issues that project managers face:

- Managing time and stress
- Managing conflict and managing difficult stakeholders
- Communicating and influencing stakeholders and senior managers
- Getting others to listen and staying in control

MANY ROLES OF THE PROJECT MANAGER

Project managers take on many roles. This includes being an integrator and coordinator for all activities on a project, negotiating amongst stakeholders, leading and motivating, and problem solving. Simply put, the project manager is a communicator, integrator, team leader, and decision-maker.

The major responsibilities of the project manager include the following:

- Set well-defined objectives using the SMART principle (specific, measurable, assignable, realistic, and time-based).
- Manage the planning, organizing, executing, controlling, and reporting of the project through all phases to ensure successful implementation.
- Develop and coordinate resources.
- Communicate across the organizational hierarchy and with stakeholders.
- Motivate and nurture team members by providing feedback, coaching, and rewards.
- Evaluate risks to senior management and manage those risks effectively throughout the project life cycle.
- Secure resources by influencing the stakeholder and through negotiation and persuasion.

Upon careful analysis of the various roles, it is easy to see why 80 to 90 percent of the time the project manager functions as a communicator. This fact should resolve the debate that exists in some technical organizations involved in project management—should the project manager have more people skills or technical skills? While it is desirable to have a manager who is strong on people skills *and* technical skills, the most valuable attributes are strong communication and people skills.

Project Manager and Power

Fifty years ago, French and Raven identified the ways in which power may be exerted. They classified power into the following five categories: expert power, legitimate power, reward power, coercive power, and referent power.

Let us expand their classification from the perspective of a project manager. If the team believes that their project manager possesses superior project-related skills and abilities, then the project manager is said to exert expert power. Legitimate power stems from the project manager's assignment to the role by upper management and gives the right to demand duty and timely completion of project tasks. Reward power is the perception by the team members that their project manager controls important resources and rewards and is willing to dispense them as appropriate. Coercive power is the capacity to punish team members that do not comply with requests or demands. Finally, referent power can be derived by identifying with, admiring, and respecting a power holder (e.g., a senior executive). Team members in turn may identify with the project manager possessing referent power.

It is worthwhile to suggest that while the project manager can wield coercive or legitimate power, he or she can probably achieve more success by inspiring the team to higher levels of achievement by setting a good example and motivating them through self-actualization.

CONFLICT MANAGEMENT

Almost all project managers will encounter conflict within their teams. Before we begin this section, we must note that the modern view of conflict is that it is not necessarily bad. Conflict is natural in all organizations due to different values. A finance department might be interested in lower inventory and the project manager might want higher inventory on hand (just in case the next shipment is delayed.

Conflicts can create deeper understanding and respect, but the more common outcome is that conflicts are destructive and harmful. How you resolve the conflict is a critical factor in determining whether the project environment will be healthy or not.

There are many symptoms of conflict. In a project, they would include the following:

- The team members preferring to work in isolation
- Finding yourself unable to make decisions at critical points
- A lack of enthusiasm and low team morale among the team members

While the project manager should play a key role in guiding the team, it's a good strategy to let the team solve the problem instead of imposing a solution upon them.

The following are possible strategies to resolve conflicts:

- Avoidance: You do not confront the problem and choose to ignore it, hoping it will go away. But by avoiding conflict altogether, you address neither the project's best interest nor the best interests of the people involved. If you have no authority to resolve the conflict, you might want to use avoidance.
- Forcing: The project manager is autocratic and communicates "my way or the highway." While this may provide short-term solutions, it rarely provides a lasting one.
- Smoothing: Here we emphasize the points of agreements and don't highlight the areas of disagreement. This does not resolve the conflict, but seeks to maintain a harmonious environment for the time being.
- Compromising: This is viewed as a "lose-lose" solution. The project manager attempts to find a middle ground in the conflict. Overuse of compromising as a strategy may deprive you of respect and the power you need to influence future outcomes. Compromise is considered appropriate when the parties are strongly committed to mutually exclusive objectives.
- Confrontation and problem solving: This is the best strategy for resolving conflicts and provides a lasting solution. Confrontation brings out

the issues and allows the manager to negotiate a lasting solution. Since all project managers will encounter conflicts at some point we will describe this in greater detail in the next section.

- Negotiation: Conflict negotiation refers to a voluntary, two-way communication in which parties involved control both the process and the outcome. Good principled negotiation involves the following actions: separate the people from the problem, dig deeper and focus on the interest of the people involved in the conflict, and invent a new solution of mutual gain.

We all get wrapped up in conflicts, but we often have no idea how to resolve them. Through self-education and experience, you can obtain the following skills necessary to resolve real-life conflict situations:

- Solving problems by negotiating the issues more frequently to a win-win conclusion
- Working together as a team more effectively, especially wherever conflict might flair in the future

In *Building Team Power*, Thomas Kayser recommends six steps for achieving win-win solutions; the process is described below:

1. Defining and selecting the problem: As a team, you specify the problem but don't include causes or solutions yet. At this stage, positions are defined by the conflicting parties. Positions are things that have been decided as a way to settle the difference. Example: "Finance Department is the real problem."

2. Analyzing the problem: The specific problem is reviewed for accuracy. Evidence, data analysis, or research must confirm that the problem is real. Don't focus on the positions presented by the parties; instead identify and prioritize possible causes for the problem. Positions don't serve the real interest of parties in dispute. They also limit creative options to solve the dispute.

3. Generating potential solutions: This is typically done with brainstorming, and you research, design, and generate two or more potential

solutions. Keeping an open mind and creativity are important in this step.

4. Selecting and planning the solution: Team members evaluate all solutions before deciding which one to select. A good strategy for problem solving is to focus on common interests. Example: "Enhancing the quality or reputation of the program." This gets to the heart of the issue, moves people beyond polarized positions, and sets the stage for mutual understanding.

5. Implementing the solution: The solution is ratified and implemented. This step might result in additional decision-making and implementation of an alternate yet related solution.

6. Evaluating the solution: Here we determine if the problem is solved, and if it was not solved, was it due to a weakness in the problem-solving process or the occurrence of some other issue?

The following is a good table to use for conflict resolution. The problem, preferred state, and common ground are documented first, followed by brainstorming of various options and consequences.

Table 8.5 Conflict Resolution Options

Conflict participants	Name: Management	Name: Vendor
Problem	Job has not been completed, so vendor should not be paid for upgrades	Since the laptops have not arrived on time from the remote staff—they are unable to get the Vista upgrade done.
Preferred solution	No payment until job is completed.	Vendors want full payment.
Common ground: Both recognize that the remote staff's travel schedules are erratic. They also recognize that some of the upgrades are successfully completed.		

Table 8.5 (*continued*)

	Suggested solutions	Impact of the solution
1.	Extend the contract	Late upgrades and disappointed users and contractor.
2.	Partial Payments based on percentage complete	Earlier distribution of funds to contractors

Team members make notes on the following questions during conflict resolution: What was the conflict about? How do you know it was a conflict? What approaches were used to resolve the conflict (withdrawing, forcing, smoothing, compromising, and confrontation)? What were the results of the above approaches? If the conflict is not resolved, are there other approaches that can produce results?

PROJECT MANAGEMENT IN ACTION

Project "MLB in Japan" Hits a Wall

To attract more fans to baseball and to generate more revenues, Major League Baseball planned a season opener between the Boston Red Sox and the Oakland A's in Japan, planned for March 25–26, 2008. This multimillion dollar adventure almost came to a screeching halt on March 19, 2008, the day before the scheduled trip.

Manager Terry Francona had told Red Sox coaches they would receive a $40,000 stipend, then discovered otherwise. "For most of the staff, this money is a big deal, as it is equivalent to two-fifths of their salary for the year," said Francona. Red Sox players, in a show of unity with the coaches and support personnel, declined to make the trip. The *Boston Globe* also added that the expectations were the same for the Oakland team. Commenting on the coaching staff, Oakland closer Huston Street said, "They're just as much a part of this team as anybody. Playoff shares, coaches get an equal share. You look at previous Japan trips, coaches have gotten an equal share."

The Players Association had negotiated a payment for each player. However, the payments to the manager, coaches, and support staff were not included in the written agreement. The Red Sox players were furious that the coaches were left out of the deal. Further exacerbating the situation, the information about the coaches was not communicated until the day before the historic flight to Japan. The union said it was merely something that fell through the cracks—something that was said during negotiations but not put into writing.

When Kevin Youkilis, a Red Sox player, was asked who was responsible for the poor communications, he said, "When you have those conference calls, you need to get it in writing. That's something we will address in our next union meeting."

Conflict Resolution in Action

A multimillion dollar prestige project was at stake. A lot of sunk costs had already been incurred. Active communication and conflict resolution was in place to make sure that the trip would not be jeopardized. Several solutions were suggested and investigated, and eventually one was chosen. According to Jackie MacMullan of the *Boston Globe*, at 4:20 P.M., just hours before the departure, conflict resolution solutions started appearing.

Red Sox ownership agreed to underwrite a portion of the estimated $600,000 required to cover Boston's coaches, staff, and trainers. The ownership was planning to recoup some of that expense from MLB and/or the Players Association. Revenues from ticket sales in Japan were brought into the equation. The players were happy with this suggested solution. All would be well—soon the Red Sox and the A's would be off to Japan to play as scheduled.

Note: The same problem had occurred once before when the Yankees went overseas for a baseball game. The solution back then was that the players would share the revenues with the coaching staff and personnel.

A sad reality of project management is that unless lessons are learned and documented, the same mistakes are likely to be made over and over again! This case study also underscores another fact about communication; the project manager must communicate the key issues to everyone using more than one method (e.g., formal verbal and formal written communication).

TEST YOURSELF

1. Management literature documents five power types: reward, expert, legitimate, coercive, and referent. Comment on which power types will work well for a project manager and which will not.

2. Comment on how you would manage a project manager who believes in constant supervision.

3. If you are a team member and you could only pick one set of attributes for a project manager—either being good at the people side of managing projects or being good at the technical side—which would you prefer? Why?

4. There is a conflict between two project participants, Joe and Mary, about the importance of prototyping in the project. Joe feels that a complete prototype must be built before development begins because the technology is untried and risky. Mary says that there is no time to prototype, and building a prototype will impact the schedule. Mary feels that the problems can be solved by consulting outside sources and that the issues likely to arise have been solved before. Assuming that there is no budget to outsource this problem, identify three possible solutions to resolve this conflict, and recommend the best one from your perspective.

KEY POINTS TO REMEMBER

- A communications management plan is a document that provides the following:
  - A collection and filing structure which details what methods will be used to gather and store various types of information.
  - A distribution structure which details to whom information (status reports, data, schedule, technical documentation, etc.) will flow and what methods (written reports, meetings, etc.) will be used to distribute various types of information.
  - A description of the information to be distributed, including format, content, level of detail, and conventions/definitions to be used
  - Production schedules showing when each type of communication will be produced

- A basic communication plan deals with:
  - What is being communicated?
  - Why is it being communicated?
  - Whom is it being communicated to?
  - How is it being communicated?
  - When will it be communicated?

- Stakeholders are anyone whose interests may be positively or negatively impacted by the project.

- Communications management involves the following:
  - Sixty to 90 percent of the time is spent on communications (in various forms).
  - A project manager (PM) is the integrator for the majority of the communication taking place during the project.

- The kickoff meeting provides a critical first impression of the project manager and the way the project will be conducted. It is also a good opportunity for the team to get to know each other.

- Effective project team meetings are essential to achieve goals.

- Communication model involves: sender, receiver, message, and medium. Communication process: Send, filter, receive, and understand.

Project Cost Estimation

INTRODUCTION

Poor cost estimating is a major source of problems and risks in a project. Often, a project manager has to commit to a cost estimate early on in the project life cycle, and once this estimate is given, it is *cast in stone*. Subsequently, during the project planning stage, as the project scope gets refined, the work is typically increased as the team understands the problem more clearly. The project manager, however, is usually unable to revise the budget to accommodate this increase in scope. Due to the triple constraint model we talked about earlier, something has to give—it could be quality, schedule, or the cost itself. As a result, it is not uncommon for projects to experience cost growth and overshoot their budgets. The ominous words "the project is way over budget" is frequently heard in most organizations! This chapter provides methods and approaches for estimating project effort and costs.

WHAT'S AHEAD

- Early estimation
  - Understand methods for top-down estimating, such as Delphi, parametric, and three-point estimation
  - Understand the difference between effort and duration

- Planning phase estimation
  - WBS: Bottom-up estimation
- Understand the process of creating and controlling cost budgets
- Rules of thumb for estimating and scheduling
- Project cost budgeting

IN THE REAL WORLD

The city of Boston had a $2.8 billion order-of-magnitude estimate to build a new tunnel and upgrade the street infrastructure. Today, the Big Dig project has already cost more than $14 billion. While this project is truly complex in scope, and a significant amount of effort was put in by all parties, it is considered to be a good case study for project cost estimation. How can a project with an initial estimate of $3 billion wind up at $15 billion? Was the scope of the project not considered fully? Risk management not performed completely? Quality issues not assessed? Was contingency planning grossly inadequate?

KEY CONCEPTS

PROJECT COST MANAGEMENT

Project cost estimation is a key process inside the knowledge area of project cost management. So let us first understand the important concepts behind project cost management. According to the PMBOK, the processes in cost management are the following:

- Cost estimating: A process used to develop an approximation of the costs needed to complete all project activities
- Cost budgeting: A cost baseline created by aggregating the estimated costs of individual activities or work packages
- Cost control: Cost variances and changes to the project budget are controlled in this process.

These processes are followed by cost budgeting. The focus of this chapter is on project cost estimation, but we cover cost budgeting briefly as well.

Figure 9.1 Cost Estimating Inputs, Tools, and Outputs

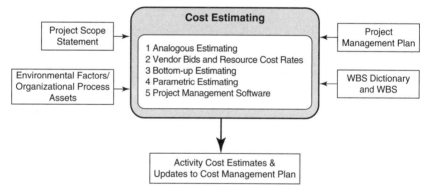

COST ESTIMATING

There are different ways to estimate the costs of a project depending on the application domain. Estimating the cost of building a house is different than estimating the cost of developing software and completely different than estimating the costs of developing a new drug. The core concepts, however, are relevant to all application domains. Cost estimation can occur as soon as a work breakdown structure has been created. In this chapter, you will see various techniques to estimate the following:

- Duration estimate for the work to be done. This is typically in units of hours, days, or weeks.

- Cost estimate for the work to be done. This includes two types of costs: labor costs (including overhead) and resource costs, such as equipment rental, training costs, and documentation costs.

- Effort estimate for the work to be done. This refers to the number of person-hours or work-hours it takes to do a task or the project itself.

From the Experience Vault

Estimating a task effort in person-hours will frequently result in optimistic estimates. Assume that a task is budgeted to take four person-hours—this will translate to half-a-day duration when entered in scheduling software if one person is working on it. But in reality, there are all kinds of interruptions and communication issues that prevent most of us from working productively for even four hours in a day. So the four-person-hour effort should probably be adjusted to a one-day duration to reduce estimation errors.

TYPES OF ESTIMATES

It is always good practice to label and communicate the type of estimate generated by a project manager, since different types of estimates are produced for the different stages of the project. The following table identifies the project life cycle and the three types of estimates.

Table 9.1 Estimate Types for Three Process Groups

Project Process Group	Type of Estimate	Relevant Strategy
Initiating	Order of magnitude	Top-down
Planning	Budget estimate	Top-down or Bottom-up
Executing	Definitive estimate	Bottom-up

Table 9.2 Estimate Accuracy

Type of Estimate	Level of Accuracy
Order of magnitude	−25% to +75%
Budget estimate	−10% to +25%
Definitive estimate	−5% to +10%

The type of estimate and the level of accuracy are summarized in table 9.2.

Next, we'll describe each type of estimate, followed by the tools and techniques used in the relevant strategy.

Order of Magnitude

The order of magnitude estimate can be generated when the preliminary scope statement has been created. This estimate provides a baseline for the project. It gives the project manager parameters within which the entire project is being funded. Unfortunately, this estimate typically gets cast in stone, and revising this estimate upward will result in resistance from the customer.

The project manager must clearly communicate to all stakeholders the parameters on which this estimate is based. For example, the estimate for the cost of a house may be in terms of the square footage. However, the parameter (i.e., cost per square foot) will depend on many assumptions, such as the location, the type of house, the quality of the builder's work, etc. For the order of magnitude to be realistic, the preliminary scope statement must be realistically assessed, verified, and all issues and assumptions acknowledged by all stakeholders. The level of accuracy for an order of magnitude estimate may vary depending on the type of industry for which the estimate is being generated.

For small to medium software projects, the level of accuracy is substantially less than in small to medium construction projects, as there is more unstructured and creative product development activity taking place. A rule of thumb that one can use is shown in figure 9.2.

Typically, the actual time, effort, or cost estimate for an order of magnitude estimate has a level of accuracy that varies between −25 percent to +75 percent. So if your project is estimated at $100,000, the final actual cost may be anywhere between $75,000 and $175,000.

Budget Estimate

The budget estimate comes out of the planning process and is more reliable than the order of magnitude estimate. This estimate typically has an accuracy that varies between −10 percent to +25 percent. So if your project is estimated at $100,000, the final cost may be anywhere between $90,000 and $125,000.

Definitive Estimate

This estimate is generated during the latter stages of execution phase of the project and is very useful to the project manager and customer, as it reliably communicates the final cost and schedule for the product. Depending on when it was created, the strategy has a level of accuracy that typically varies between −5 percent to +10 percent. So if your project is estimated at $100,000, the final actual estimate may be anywhere between $95,000 and $110,000.

Figure 9.2 Estimates and Their Accuracy Over Time

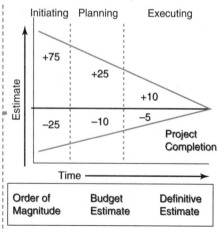

We summarize the various levels of accuracy in the figure 9.2. As the project proceeds, the cost and schedule estimates become more accurate. A general rule of thumb is that 50 percent of the way through the project, the cost estimate is usually quite accurate.

Next, we'll examine the relevant strategies and various real-world tools that can be used to make the three types of estimates introduced above. They can be classified according to two broad categories: top-down and bottom-up estimating techniques.

TOP-DOWN AND BOTTOM-UP ESTIMATING

With top-down estimation, you focus on the overall development process and don't necessarily break the project down into very detailed activities. The estimate is often in terms of high-level project parameters. This allows for quick estimation of the project effort.

In bottom-up estimation, you focus on individual project activities and require a detailed breakdown, typically the WBS activities and work packages. You roll up the numbers of the lower-level activities to come up with an estimate for the entire project.

Top-Down Estimation Techniques

- Delphi method
- Parametric models
- Analogous historical data
- Three-point technique

Analogous Historical Data

Estimation by analogy is a popular method for estimating projects. In this method, you compare the proposed project with previous projects that are judged to be similar. It is a simple and effective approach when there are detailed metrics about previous projects, which can be compared to those of the new project. The process also requires experienced people to be available who remember the historical data accurately and can comment on the merit of the similarity assumptions. If bottom-up estimating is being performed, you must carefully compare individual activity estimates with those of the historical activities.

Delphi Method

This is a group-based technique for producing estimates, originally developed in the 1950s by the RAND Corporation. If one were to ask a group of experts to provide estimates for any quantity, it is assumed that they will eventually arrive at the same, correct estimate. The process is time-consuming because it may take several iterations. This technique provides a formal, structured approach for the development of estimates. It can be used even when no historical data exists. The Delphi technique has been shown to be a satisfactory approach for estimating. The technique is based on the following ideas:

- Extreme views get annulled or get corrected to a good mean.
- It is anonymous—participants do not reveal their identity to other estimators since such estimates are susceptible to bias and intimidation.

With this technique, the project manager chooses an estimation team and waits until that team arrives at a consensus on the estimate. There are typically three rounds of estimates, and it seems that with each Delphi iteration, the variance is reduced and the accuracy of the estimate is improved.

The Delphi moderator is anyone who is familiar with the Delphi process and able to lead the estimation session, but who does not have a stake in it. The project manager should not be the monitor, as he/she is most likely a part of the estimation team. A template that can be used for Delphi estimation is illustrated in figure 9.3.

As each participant observes the estimates of the other participants, he or she typically seeks clarification about the project scope and revises the estimate for the next round. The variance declines; and therefore, this process results in a fairly accurate estimate. The project manager ultimately uses the results at the final meeting and compiles the scope, estimates, and assumptions from each member.

Figure 9.3 Delphi Template

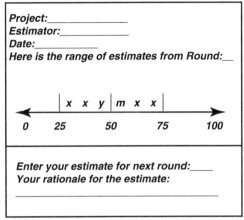

x = Delphi member estimates
Y = Your estimate
M = Median

Parametric Model

These are mathematical models that use project characteristics to compute a total project estimate. This is a quick way to obtain an estimate. When facing an estimating task, the estimator always has a model in mind. This intuitive model can be formally established as a cost model.

Most, if not all, cost models use predictors. According to Tom De Marco, a leader in the theory and practice of software development, "A predictor is an early noted metric that has a strong correlation to some later results."

Most cost estimating tools have a parametric model inside. Parametric models consist of equations and parameters. The values of the parameters are determined by assumptions and calibrated using historical data. Let us look at some simple models:

In a certain town, a residential house costs $100 per square foot. This parametric equation was generated from historic sales data.

As a construction industry project manager, you are trying to estimate the price at which you can sell a 2,500 square foot house that you are planning to build.

$$\text{Estimated Cost} = 2{,}500 \times \$100 = \$\,250{,}000$$

In this example, the $100 per square foot is the parameter. The equation is for the estimated cost and contains the parameter. The parameter was determined from historical data on housing sales in the past. The types of questions one can ask about the value of the parameter might typically include the following:

- How many years of data were included?
- What are the boundaries of the area used?
- What is the spread in the prices, and what are the error bounds?

Three-Point Technique

Practicing project managers rely on a three-point technique, also called the PERT Weighted Average or PERT Mean to estimate efforts and costs. In this technique, we use three data points. For example, if we are considering estimating a schedule, then these are the data points:

- Pessimistic estimate (P). The pessimistic estimate is used to come up with a worst-case scenario—if all the risks materialize and everything that could go wrong did go wrong, but the project was still completed. If the project was repeated, 1 percent of the time this would be the schedule.
- Most likely estimate (L).
- Optimistic estimate (O). The optimistic time is defined as the shortest duration one has had or might expect to experience, given that everything happens as expected. If the project was repeated, 1 percent of the time this would be the schedule.

This is the formula to calculate the PERT Mean:

$$M = (P + 4 \times L + O) / 6$$

Example: Suppose that we are trying to estimate the duration to build a prototype. Pessimistically, if things go wrong, we estimate that this will take 20 days. Optimistically, the prototype can be completed in 4 days. Most likely the prototyping will take 6 days.

Figure 9.4 Optimistic, Likely, and Pessimistic Estimates, with the PERT Mean

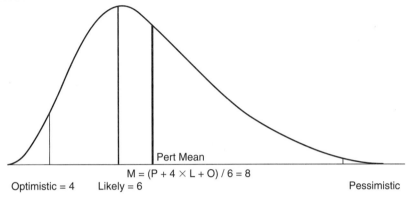

Substitute these numbers in the following equation:

$$M = (P + 4 \times L + O) / 6$$
$$= (20 + 4 \times 6 + 4) / 6 = 48 / 6$$
$$M = 8 \text{ days}$$

This results in a mean of eight days, which can be used as the activity duration estimate for the project.

The following formula is useful for determining the standard deviation. You should use this with the PERT Mean to determine how diverse the estimates are and to assign some degree of confidence to the estimates. The formula approximates the real standard deviation formula, but it is accurate enough and its simplicity makes it useful.

Standard Deviation, σ = (Pessimistic – Optimistic) / 6

For the above example, we have:

$$\sigma = (20 - 4) / 6 = 2.7 \text{ days}$$

Therefore, we would quote the estimate as: 8 ± 3 days. The confidence intervals for σ are as follows:

$1\sigma = 68.2\%$ The final result has a 68% chance to be within 8 ± 3 days.

$2\sigma = 95.5\%$ The final result has a 96% chance to be within 8 ± 6 days.

$3\sigma = 99.7\%$ The final result has a 99.7% chance to be within 8 ± 9 days.

So if you would like to have a 96 percent confidence estimate for the project, you would quote the following number:

The project estimate is 8 ± 6 days with 96 percent confidence.

BOTTOM-UP ESTIMATION

This approach to estimation involves first constructing a work breakdown structure. This provides an opportunity for the project manager and team members to precisely estimate individual activities and work packages.

The bottom-up budgeting approach is generally considered to be more accurate than top-down estimation methods, as the scope of the project is refined in a highly detailed manner. This generates an accurate compilation of effort and costs. The risk is that it is possible for the project manager to be so focused on the project details that he or she might miss out on some key cost elements of the project.

There was a popular report in the press about a decade ago about a building contractor in Connecticut who had an exceptionally precise estimate for a new government building—but he had not included sophisticated excavation costs in the bid. The government refused to reopen the bid or to cancel the contract despite the fact that an entire component of the project was omitted. This case proves that the most effective approach to estimating is to combine the top-down with the bottom-up estimation technique.

Example

For our sample case study about migrating from Windows XP to Vista, we illustrate the first few activities that have been estimated using the bottom-up technique. We see in figure 9.5 that the initiation phase takes 3 days, the planning phase takes 13 days, and the project-to-date activity has been estimated at 16 days.

Figure 9.5 Vista Project Migration Activity Estimates

⊹	❶	Task Name	Duration
1		− XP to Vista Migration	16 days
2		− Initiation	3 days
3		Project kickoff	1 day
4		Obtain stakeholder approval	2 days
5		− Planning	13 days
6		Examine project feasibility	4 days
7		Create project plan	4 days
8		Do mock-up test	5 days

Applying PERT Weights to Refine Bottom-Up Estimates

Just as we used the three-point method to estimate the project, we can use the PERT weights to refine the bottom-up estimates shown in the above example. First, we provide the optimistic, expected, and pessimistic durations. For tasks 3, 4, 6, 7, and 8, the optimistic, expected, and pessimistic durations are listed in figure 9.6.

Figure 9.6 Vista Project Migration Optimistic, Pessimistic, and Likely Activity Duration Estimates

	Task Name	Duration	Optimistic Dur.	Expected Dur.	Pessimistic Dur.
1	− XP to Vista Migration	16 days	15 days	16 days	17 days
2	− Initiation	3 days	2days	3 days	4 days
3	Project kickoff	1 day	1 day	1 day	3 days
4	Obtain stakeholder approval	2 days	1 day	2 days	3 days
5	− Planning	13 days	13 days	13 days	13 days
6	Examine project fea	4 days	1 day	4 days	8 days
7	Create project plan	4 days	1 day	4 days	8 days

After this has been accomplished, you can use the PERT formula to come up with revised estimates if needed. The project optimistically has a duration of 15 days as figure 9.6 illustrates. Similarly, you can view likely and pessimistic estimates.

Figure 9.7 Vista Project Migration Duration Estimates

❶	Task Name	Opt. Dur.	Opt. Start	Opt. Finish
1	⊟ XP to Vista Migration	15 days	Mon 3/10/08	Fri 3/28/08
2	⊟ Initiation	2 days	Mon 3/10/08	Tue 3/11/08
3	Project kickoff	1 day	Mon 3/10/08	Mon 3/10/08
4	Obtain stakeholder approval	1 day	Tue 3/11/08	Tue 3/11/08
5	⊟ Planning	13 days	Wed 3/12/08	Fri 3/28/08
6	Examine project feasibility	1 day	Wed 3/12/08	Mon 3/17/08
7	Create project plan	1 day	Tue 3/18/08	Fri 3/21/08
8	Do mock-up test	1 day	Mon 3/24/08	Fri 3/28/08

> Do not add extra slack time to your bottom-up estimates. Instead, use the PERT weights to generate optimistic, likely, and pessimistic estimates to generate a range of dates.

COST BUDGETING

Once you have completed the cost estimate, you can begin cost budgeting. This is where you assign costs to activities in the WBS. The biggest expense on most projects is the cost of labor or resource effort. A project uses many different kinds of resources, which include people, facilities, materials, equipment, and other administrative expenses. They are summarized below:

- Labor: Wages paid to staff; obtained by simply multiplying the work-hours estimated by the resource rate

- Overhead: Cost of payroll taxes and fringe benefits; usually a percentage of labor

- Materials: Items used in the project; cement, lumber, paint

- Supplies: Cost of tools, office supplies, equipment; should be prorated if expected life is beyond the project

- General and administrative: cost of management and support services, such as, purchasing, accounting, secretarial; usually a percentage of project cost

- Equipment rental: Computers, printers, compressors, cranes, trucks

- Profit or bonus: reward for successfully completing the project; profit: calculated as a percentage of project cost

Other direct and indirect expenses can be added to the project budget, including one-time expenses, such as travel and training. Project managers must also be aware of hidden costs and must allow for them in a risk analysis.

Expenses for the final budget can be validated using data from historic templates if available, such as the example shown in table 9.3 for a generic project life cycle. The company knows that in the past it has typically spent about 5 percent on the initiation phase, 20 percent on planning, etc. For a project estimated at $100,000, the initiating phase is projected to cost $5,000. This broader view is called life-cycle costing.

Table 9.3 Life Cycle–Based Cost Distribution Estimates

Project Phase	Cost Distribution	Budget Allocation
Initiating	5%	$5,000
Planning	20%	$20,000
Executing	70%	$70,000
Closing	5%	$5,000
Total	**100%**	**$100,000**

ESTIMATING FRAMEWORK—SUMMARY

Let us summarize the estimation concepts using an estimating framework. Figure 9.8 explains the estimating framework and is a useful summary of this chapter.

1. First, Top-Down

    The project scope is used to size the project. The scope is the basis of the estimate in person-hours/days and answers the question, "How big is the project?" Team members help to generate the estimates, but the manager should not entirely trust the team's estimates. Depending on the personality and experience of the team member, the project manager may receive very optimistic or pessimistic estimates. The project manager must attempt to consider all factors that will affect the project's effort. The goal is to develop a practical estimate. For example, staff productivity may be estimated from data from historical records or from experience. Parametric models or other techniques can also be used to identify the project effort.

2. Next, Bottom-Up

    At this point, the team should create a bottom-up estimate using the WBS and should enter the activities and resources information into project management software. This will generate the project schedule. A good rule of thumb is to decompose a project into activities using the rule of "one to two people for one to two weeks." This rule says that no activity should be either too short or too long. Tasks of very short duration add unnecessarily to project management bureaucracy, and long duration activities are more inaccurate in their estimates.

3. Do Cost Budgeting

    The planned cost for the project is developed by adding in resource rates, facilities, materials, equipment, and other administrative expenses.

4. Check Estimates and Budgets

    To develop effective budgets and estimates, you must cross-check and adjust top-down and bottom-up estimating techniques. These adjustments produce the most reliable effort and cost estimates for your project.

5. Update Your Historical Records

    When the project is over, you must update the historical records. Even updating the "actuals" inside your project management software or your spreadsheet will result in more reliable estimates and budgets for the company's future projects.

Figure 9.8 Estimating Framework

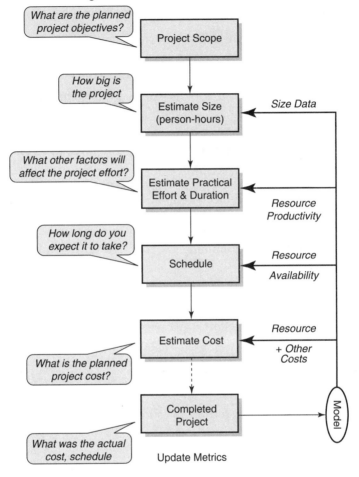

PM PROJECT MANAGEMENT IN ACTION

4GT Model

The 4GT model was researched and developed by the author (Vijay Kana-bar) using research data primarily from Oracle applications at the Great-West Life Insurance Assurance Company in Winnipeg, Canada. The model estimates the efforts of small database-driven and Web-based applications. It involves three predictors: the number of forms, the number of entities or tables, and reports. Recall that a predictor is an early metric that co-relates with final estimates. The parametric model for estimating programming effort is illustrated using two equations.

Equation 1: Programming Effort = (10.2 × # of forms) + (7.9 × # of reports) + (4.9 × # of entities)

The 4GT model uses person-hours as a unit. Example:
A proposed telephone system has 5 forms, 2 reports, and 3 tables.
Implementation: Oracle RDBMS

$$\text{Programming Effort} = 10.2 \times 5 + 7.9 \times 2 + 4.9 \times 3$$
$$= 252 \text{ Person-Hours}$$

In most projects, programming effort is one third of total life cycle development effort.

Equation 2: Project Effort = 3.1 × Programming Effort

The total estimated project effort = 781 person-hours.

TEST YOURSELF

1. Which is more accurate: top-down estimation or bottom-up estimation? Why?

2. What are the advantages of the various methods introduced for top-down estimation?

3. What are the strengths of parametric models? What are the weaknesses? List two of each.

4. You are asked to give almost a 100 percent guarantee that a certain budget or duration estimate will be achieved. What method can you suggest to come up with such a reliable number?

KEY POINTS TO REMEMBER

- You must get the team members to provide estimates where possible.
- When doing bottom-up estimating, use the rule of "one to two people for one to two weeks."
- You can calculate the duration by dividing the total effort by the number of resources.
- You can calculate the effort by multiplying the duration by the number of resources.
- For many types of projects, it is preferable to estimate in days and not hours, as people are not productive eight hours every day.
- You should always communicate the type of estimate to the stakeholder. During the initiating phase, you only have order of magnitude estimates.
- You should consider more than one estimating tool or technique when developing estimates.
- Reliable budget estimates are arrived at only after creating a work breakdown structure.
- You must combine both the top-down and bottom-up estimating techniques for good budget estimates.
- Once you've completed cost estimation, you do cost budgeting.
- Cost control follows cost budgeting. This process involves reviewing project progress reports, comparing the results against the cost baseline, and determining if management action must be taken.)

Project Risk Management

INTRODUCTION

Risk management is recognized as a best practice in project management for reducing unexpected events. Project managers and project teams are always more optimistic than they should be. Risk management balances excessive optimism by introducing a process that constantly asks "what if?" Project risk management attempts to deal with a concern before it becomes a crisis. This improves the chances of successful project completion.

WHAT'S AHEAD

- Project risk management
  - Understanding risk management
  - Identifying typical project risks
  - The key processes in project risk management
- Risk identification
- Risk quantification
  - Qualitative and quantitative risk management
- Risk mitigation
  - Identifying risk response strategies
- Risk monitoring and control

IN THE REAL WORLD

Microsoft founder Bill Gates once described risk management in his industry. He said:

> Software development is not a typical industry. It has substantial upfront costs but low recurring costs and generous margins, a pattern that influences how we assess the risks of introducing a new product.
>
> Let's say you're in a conventional business where margins are thin and you're sure there is a margin for the product you are contemplating. For instance, say you're weighing whether to build a steel factory, which—like most manufacturing plants—will have high start-up and capital costs.
>
> It makes perfect sense to carefully analyze your costs. You know there is a market for steel, but without analysis you don't know if you're going to be competitive in providing it. If your costs end up ten percent too high, you will be sorry you built the factory.
>
> Considerations are quite different when it comes to deciding whether to build a new software product. Most of the risk doesn't concern whether you'll meet development cost targets. The risk is whether there is an adequate market at all. Our failures tend to result from markets being too small.
>
> Software companies are forced to gamble on unproved markets because it's nearly impossible to ask customers to predict whether they'll buy and use a new kind of tool. Successful software companies push the frontier of what's possible. We have no choice but to spend all the money to create a product before we sell any—and then hope there's a big market for it.
>
> It surprises me that movie studios can't spend, say, ten percent of budget to create a trailer and then do focus groups to predict how popular the movie will be and whether production should continue. That must not work or somebody would have done it by now—but it stuns me that it doesn't.

KEY CONCEPTS

As projects get more complex, risks compound, and problems are more likely to occur. As you consider whether risk management is the right solution for your company, you may want to look at some statistics. One management consulting firm reports that in a survey of its major clients, "over 35 percent admit to cost as well as schedule overruns."

- 25 percent of large projects completely fail.
- 40 percent of all types of projects are either late or fail.
- 15 percent of projects have no benefit to the organization.

Perhaps the most agonizing aspect of project failures is the knowledge that most of these failures could have been avoided. We've all seen, at one time or another, the top ten reasons for project failures:

1. Inadequate specifications
2. Changing requirements
3. Change control mismanagement
4. Inexperienced personnel
5. Unrealistic estimates
6. Subcontractor failure
7. Poor project management
8. Lack of user involvement
9. Expectations not properly set
10. Poor architectural design

These top ten reasons for project failure are nothing more than unmanaged risks. Unmanaged, they will almost always add up to failure. Why do we see the same top ten reasons time after time? After all, the list has not changed dramatically over the past 20 years.

Most companies do not have a system for identifying and managing risks. The top 10 (or even top 50) reasons for project failure are actually risks that were not identified early enough in the process to be corrected. As a result, these risks became problems. Your investment in risk management (typically two to four percent of your project costs) compares favorably with cost overruns and lost opportunity costs, which often reach more than 50 percent. So, while the investment in risk management is comparatively small, the potential gains are enormous.

PROJECT RISK MANAGEMENT

Risk management should be regarded as an integral part of the project management methodology. The purpose of risk management is both to actively predict problems that might negatively impact the project objectives and to manage the problems if they have occurred.

So how do we define risk? Webster's dictionary defines risk as "the possibility of suffering, harm, or loss" and "a factor, element, or course involving uncertain danger." We can, however, broadly define risk as both a threat—an event that may cause suffering, harm, or loss—and an opportunity—an event that may cause us to gain or profit. (The latter view is regarded as "business risk" and is not the focus of this chapter.) The former is also regarded as a "pure risk"—one that can be deflected or transferred to another party through a contract or insurance policy. There are no opportunities associated with a pure risk, only losses.

Project risk management is the art and science of identifying, quantifying, responding to, and controlling project risk. It includes maximizing the results of positive events and minimizing the consequences of adverse events. When we speak of risk, we are talking of some future event that may or may not take place. With risk, therefore, we have to talk in terms of probability of occurrence. If we are 100 percent certain that a risk event will occur, then this event is no longer a risk—it is a certain threat (or opportunity), and immediate action must be taken.

What Are the Sources of Project Risk?

We have already listed a few common sources of project risks. Risk events differ from project to project and certainly from one business application area to another. Regardless, a common thread exists. Consider the list below; do you recognize some of your risks in this list?

- Scope creep
- Insufficient resources
- Low quality
- Excessive schedule pressure
- Cost overruns
- Inadequate configuration control
- Inadequate cost estimating
- Excessive paperwork
- Error-prone software
- Excessive time to market
- Friction between contractor and client
- Not enough time
- Inadequate senior management support
- Poor communication

We note that there is a great deal of similarity between the sources of risk and the top ten reasons for project failure. It seems that risks turn into failures.

The list is not in order of importance. From our experience, poor communication and scope creep are the most common sources of risk. A good way to discover risks is to ask yourself, "What did not work well in my last project?" If you answered "project communications," then you should anticipate that risk again on your next project!

Benefits of Risk Management

Risk management has often been compared with medical practice. There are a lot of similarities between both the professions. Your family doctor places substantial emphasis on prevention. Key health indicators are monitored and tracked annually. Think about heart failure or heart attack for instance. Can steps be taken early on that detect or prevent these medical risks? If we cannot prevent them, can we contain these risks? If a person is more prone to these medical conditions, are there steps one can take to control these risks?

Many project managers have successfully demonstrated that project risks can be actively tackled and prevented. If proactive steps are taken, the costs or damage to a project is much less. A good project manager must therefore know how to recognize risks, evaluate their impact, and take steps to counter them. Other benefits of risk management are the following:

- Helps to meet objectives on schedule and on budget
- Proactive versus reactive—focuses attention on mitigation of risks ahead of time
- Helps to identify risk at its early stages and increases effectiveness of mitigation
- Up to 90 percent of project problems can be eliminated through proper risk management
- Improves morale and stakeholder satisfaction
- Provides competitive advantages

A Risk Management Example

Let us look at a sample risk management event. This example deals with a software communications company, called FTP Communications, of North Andover, Massachusetts. During the dot-com boom era, this company had a high turnover on projects. The turnover was both internal (reassignment) and external (members quitting). We interpret the probability of the risk turnover as being high. The amount at stake is also high because the project schedule is jeopardized. This leads us to believe that the risk is unacceptable, and we must identify suitable risk responses to mitigate the risks. This analysis is summarized below:

Risk: Turnover

Quantification: High impact and high probability

- Based on past history, turnover is estimated to be 50 percent—one in two team members will quit or be moved to other projects. The impact of this risk is high on project schedule and project cost.

Risk response planning:

- Meet with current staff to discuss turnover.
- Resolve factors before project starts.
- Is it possible to give out a project completion bonus?
- Define a backup staff member for every key role.
- Define higher documentation standards.
- Disperse project information widely.

If the project manager proactively investigates the above steps, it will improve the chances of project success. FTP Communications used the above techniques and also gave substantial bonuses to project team members, which resulted in successful projects.

Risk Management Process

In examining the above example, you notice that we followed certain risk management processes. The goal of risk management is to identify, quantify, and mitigate risk events before they become threats to the project. This information is documented inside your project plan. The risk management plan documents both short-term and long-term risks to the project schedule and cost, as well as to the project deliverables. Risk management is an integral part of the project quality assurance effort for minimizing the major sources of rework, schedule and cost overruns, and performance and quality degradation.

Risk management processes as introduced in the PMBOK guide are presented in figures 10.1 and 10.2. Figure 10.1 describes the first four processes.

Risk Management Planning
This process involves establishing the risk management framework for the project. The key deliverable is the risk management plan.

Project Risk Identification
This phase involves identifying risk events (such as changes in requirements, new development technologies, or inexperienced resources) that

Figure 10.1 Risk Management Processes

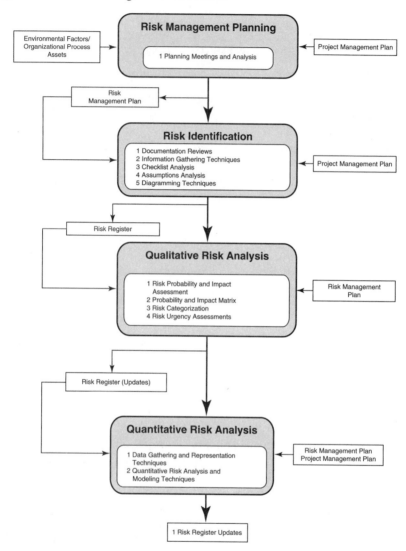

might have a significant impact on the project. These items or events might be identified through risk identification checklists, through reporting by project participants, through comparison with historical data, and through use of computer software.

Project Risk Quantification (Qualitative and Quantitative)
Using tools and techniques such as the Risk Contour Templates, Decision Analysis, Impact Analysis, Monte Carlo Schedule and Cost Analysis

Figure 10.2 Risk Management Plan

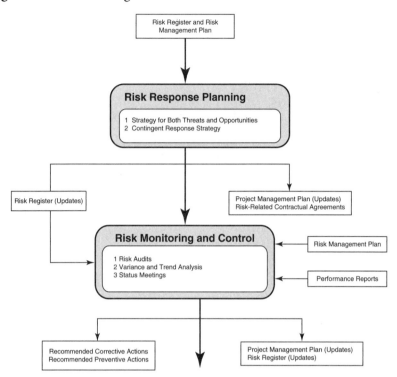

(simulation), and related techniques and models, we quantify the identified risks. Risk quantification can be broken down into qualitative risks and quantitative risks.

Figure 10.2 describes the remaining processes.

Risk Response Planning

The key risks are mitigated using techniques such as avoidance, information buying, risk transfer, and risk sharing. Risk reduction is achieved by reducing either the probability or the risk impact (amount at stake) or both.

Risk Control

Risk control involves activities such as risk management planning, risk resolution, and risk monitoring.

Risk Monitoring

Provides timely risk visibility and resolution. It incorporates techniques such as milestone tracking, tracking of top risks, and regular risk reassessment.

During this phase, the risk management plan is continuously updated as new risks are identified and addressed.

Next we will review some of the key processes in more detail.

RISK IDENTIFICATION

As risks change over time and new risks arise, this process of risk identification is repeated several times through the project's life cycle. Risk identification can be facilitated with the help of a checklist of common risk areas for your projects. Historic records of previous projects and expertise of the project managers or other experts play a key role in risk identification.

The risk management plan, which is a key input to the risk identification process, can now be updated with identified risks.

Example: If you were organizing the Olympics, you might have identified the following broad categories of risks:

- Safety: Athlete safety; VIP security
- Technology/IT: Publicity and prep communication failures
- Logistics: Delivery failures of critical items
- Ticketing: Counterfeit tickets and scalpers
- Transportation: Traffic tie-ups
- Accommodation and tourism: Standard visitors; lost passports
- Communication: Athletes and tourists speaking hundreds of languages

RISK QUANTIFICATION

The goal of risk quantification is to assess the impacts of the key risks. On a large project, you may discover several hundred risks. However, not all risks can be mitigated. So the next step is to quantify the risks so that we can then mitigate them. The guide to the PMBOK splits this process into two processes, quantitative and qualitative. We present both the analyses as follows.

Qualitative Risk Analysis

Qualitative risk analysis is done to prioritize the identified risks for further action. This analysis determines the priority of identified risks by calculating their occurrence probability and the corresponding impact on project objectives, as well as other factors such as cost, schedule, scope, and quality.

Quantitative Risk Analysis

Quantitative risk analysis is performed to assign a quantitative value for risks that have been ranked by the qualitative risk analysis process as potentially affecting the project's competing demands. This process analyzes the effect of those risk events and assigns a numerical rating to those risks, and it presents a quantitative approach to making decisions in uncertain situations.

The purpose of this activity is to:

- Quantify the possible impacts on the project and their probabilities of occurrence
- Assess the probability of completing the specific project objectives
- Identify important risks by quantifying their effects to the project
- Identify realistic and achievable cost, schedule, or scope targets in the presence of risks
- Determine the best project management decision in uncertain conditions

Even though quantitative risk analysis generally follows the qualitative risk analysis process, experienced risk managers sometimes perform it directly after risk identification.

Risks can be analyzed in two dimensions: probability (P) and amount at stake, which is a measure of the risk consequences (C). In figure 10.3, we illustrate the four quadrants to which risks can be assigned. During the qualitative analysis, we focus on the quadrant having risks with high probability and high consequence, which is the upper right-hand quadrant of figure 10.3. The project manager must focus on the upper right-hand quadrant. The risks in the other quadrants must be monitored, but the project manager need not necessarily create risk plans for them.

Figure 10.3 Risk Quantification

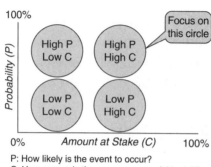

P: How likely is the event to occur?
C: How severe is the consequence of this risk?

Expected Monetary Value

Let us review two sample risk quantification tools. Expected monetary value (EMV) calculates the average outcome when the future includes scenarios that may or may not happen. For each outcome, EMV multiplies:

1. Risk event probability (P): An estimate of the probability that a given risk event will occur.

2. Risk event value, or amount at stake (A): An estimate of the gain or loss that will be incurred if the risk event does occur. The risk event value must reflect both tangibles and intangibles.

$$\text{EMV (Expected Monetary Value)} = \text{Impact} \times \text{Probability}$$

Consider the toss of a coin. Heads you will win \$100, tails you will lose \$90. We can use expected monetary value to determine if this bet is profitable for us or not.

$$\text{Expected Value (win)} = 0.50 \times \$100 = \$50$$
$$\text{Expected Value (lose)} = 0.50 \times \$90 = \$45$$

Since the expected value (the total, \$50 – \$45 = \$5) is positive \$5, this project is profitable!

Decision Tree

A decision tree is a diagram that depicts key interactions among decisions and associated chance events, as they are understood by the decision maker. It illustrates the various options schematically with probabilities. The branches of the tree represent either decisions (shown as boxes) or chance events (shown as circles).

Figure 10.4 Expected Monetary Value (EMV) Decision Tree

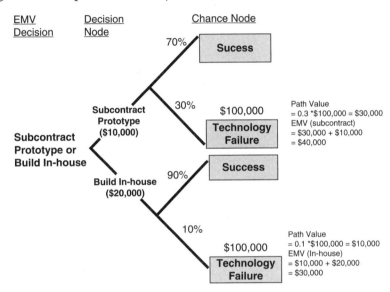

Example 2

A project manager is contemplating whether to build a prototype in house or to sub-contract it to an outside vendor. The Expected Monetary Value decision is explained in figure 10.4. The cost to build the prototype in house in $20,000, but it can be subcontracted for $10,000. There are assumed to be two outcomes as a result of the prototype effort: success and failure. e.g., the required technology is shown not to be reliable.

If the prototype is subcontracted, the project manager estimates the chance for success is 70%. If the prototype is developed in house, the project manager estimates the chance for success is 90%. In both cases, the technology failure will result in excess costs of $100,000. This might be business opportunity loss, schedule slippage, or cost overruns.

The decision tree is read as follows. The failure path value for the sub-contract option is:

$$\text{Path Value} = 0 \times \$100,000 = \$30,000$$

The EMV includes the cost of the subcontracted prototype, $10,000, so

$$\text{EMV (Subcontract)} = \$10,000 + \$30,000 = \$40,000$$

The failure path value for the build in house option is:

$$\text{Path Value} = 0.1 \times \$100,000 = \$10,000$$

The EMV includes the cost of building the prototype in house, $10,000, so

$$\text{EMV (Build in house)} = \$20,000 + \$10,000 = \$30,000$$

The build in house option has the lower EMV for the failure case, and so it is the preferred option. Even though building the prototype in house is more expensive, the costs associated with the risk of failure are much lower and make it the best option.

Most project managers will not need complex risk quantification tools and techniques. Using simple risk contours will achieve the purpose of quantifying the risks so that the project manager can move on to risk response planning.

Figure 10.5 Risk Quantification Countours

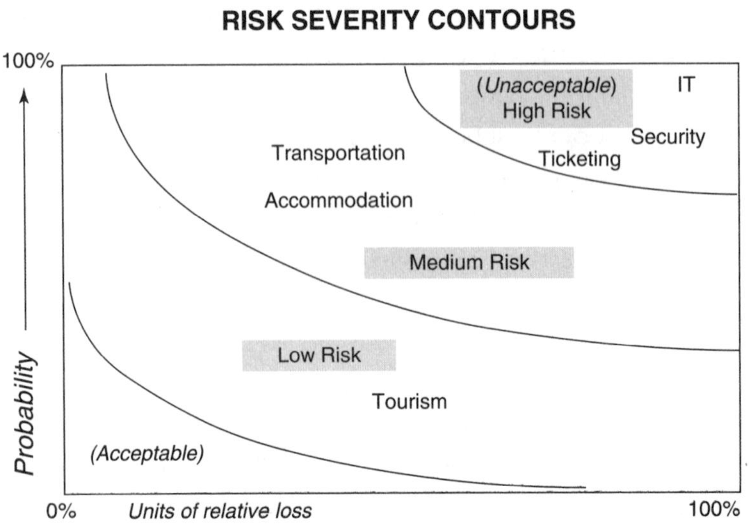

RISK SEVERITY CONTOURS

Example: For the Olympic case study, we have quantified the risks and put them into the following contours:

- High Risk: IT, ticketing, security
- Medium Risk: Transportation, accommodation
- Low Risk: Tourism

RISK RESPONSE PLANNING

Risk response planning is defined as developing procedures and techniques to enhance opportunities and reduce threats to the project's objective; the risk response plan is updated whenever a risk occurs. Strategies such as avoidance, transferance, mitigation, acceptance, and sharing are used by the project manager to mitigate the risks. A typical risk response planning document will include all the identified risks, a description of the risks, how they'll impact the project objectives, and the strategy to prevent or mitigate the risks.

Common Techniques with Examples

- Avoidance: Change the scope of the project.
- Transference: Purchase insurance.
- Mitigation: Containment—send the resource for training.
- Acceptance: Assign a contingency budget to mitigate the risk.
- Sharing: Create an equal partnership in the business.

See table 10.1 for more risk response techniques.

Example

A simple template for responding to risks, shown in table 10.2, should be used after we have quantified the key risks. For the Olympics example, we have completed one example using this template.

Table 10.1 Risk Response Techniques

Personnel shortfalls	Use top talent, team building, training, preschedule staff
Scope not clear	Prototype application
Outsourcing risks	Check references, pre-award audits, award-fee contracts, site visits, colocation of team
Unrealistic schedule	Incremental development

Table 10.2 Risk Mitigation Template

Risk Event	Impact of Risk	Prevention/Containment/Mitigation Strategy
Ticketing	Customers and revenues	We should test the IT system to make sure that ticketing works. For customers who don't have access to a computer, a toll-free number will be provided.

RISK MONITORING AND CONTROL

The previous processes focused on the planning aspects of risk management. Once the project is underway, however, we have to actively track and control project risks. Why? It is important to understand that even the most thorough and comprehensive analysis by the best project managers and project teams cannot identify all risks. So this process of constantly performing risk analysis is very important. Once new risks are identified, we update the risk management plan.

Risk Reporting at Status Meetings

A complete list of all risks identified should be made available to the project team at all times. The project plan should also document risk management details. Spending five minutes at each project team meeting to brief members and to update the risk management plan is a good strategy. The discussion pertaining to project risk analysis should involve the following topics:

- Risk area and description
- Rationale behind the risk
- Management action required
- Management plan to remove risk
- How long this item has been a risk
- Risk tracking plan

The template shown in figure 10.6 can be useful for tracking and controlling individual risk events.

Figure 10.6 Risk Item Tracking Form

Risk Item Tracking Form

Risk Identifier: _A-101_ Status: _Open_ Date: 2/1/09_

Severity: (H) | Risk: Schedule _X_ Technical: _ Cost: __X__

Risk Item Description:
External staff are not getting the laptops
in house for upgrades in a timely manner

Mitigation Plan:
Communicate travel status to contractors an IT.
Communicate open availability slots to external
staff for possible upgrades

Start Date: _2/1/09___**Completion Date:** _2/15/09___

Responsible Manager: ___Joe King_____

Mitigation Plan Status:
Mitigation plan underdevelopment.

A summary report for the above should be maintained and managed by the project manager.

COMMUNICATING RISKS TO SENIOR MANAGEMENT

A major purpose of risk management is to communicate risks to key stakeholders. In this context, reporting risks to senior management is essential. Some organizations require both development of an executive summary (for reporting purposes) and presentation of the executive summary (formally).

Develop Executive Summary

After the risk management plan is completed, a one-page executive summary should be prepared, including the most significant risks which confront the project and the business unit. In other words, what keeps you up at night? Some things to include in the summary are:

- Major risks and risk responses to contain these risks
- Open action items resulting from the risk management review
- Contingency plans
- Conclusion about overall risks

Present Executive Summary

Some organizations require a presentation of the executive summary and related documentation. Check with your manager or risk management coordinator to determine whether this is a required step for your organization. When communicating with senior management, some useful guidelines to remember are the following:

- Show only a summary of the key risks.
- Excessive information is useless.
- A one-page summary is sufficient.
- Briefly communicate:
  - Management action required
  - Management plan to remove risk

TOP-DOWN VERSUS BOTTOM-UP RISK MANAGEMENT

The previous examples focused on identifying risks from a top-down perspective. The United States Department of Defense (DoD) suggests the following categories for top-down risk identification:

- Technical
- Program
- Support
- Schedule
- Cost

However, after a WBS has been constructed it is desirable to do a bottom-up risk analysis. Here is a list of sample bottom-up risks:

- Schedule
  - Task with duration greater than three weeks
  - Task dependent on external parties
  - Task estimated optimistically
  - Task involving new vendor
  - Tasks with start-to-start dependency
- Scope
  - Tasks involving functionality that is not clear
  - Tasks with dependency on unavailable tools and technology

The bottom-up method is only useful if the project plan is complete. Notice figure 10.7. All it takes is to add a simple column in your scheduling software or spreadsheet to flag a task as a risk. In figure 10.7, we have identified certain tasks as risks so the project manager can keep an eye on them.

RISK MANAGEMENT IN ACTION

This case study pertains to the historic 100th Boston Marathon which, in 1996, was the world's largest marathon. For the project manager, the race director, and other members of the project team, this was a huge project

Figure 10.7 Bottom-Up Risk Tracking

	Name	Risk?	Comments	Dur	Work	Res. Init.	Start
42	Update Project Workbook			5d	2d	PM	2/15/96
43	**Obtain Approvals**			1d	0.5d		2/15/96
44	Request TPC Funding Approval			1d	0.5d	PM	2/15/96
45	**Development phase**			110d	636..2d		2/15/96
46	**Build solution**			110d	6.7.75d		2/15/96
47	Acquire Permits	Y		10 d	3d	BS	2/1/96
48	**Acquire Support Resources**			100d	14d		2/29/96
49	Order Signage	Y	BKB delays	40d	4d	BS	2/29/96
50	Order Furniture			40d	4d	BS	4/25/96
51	Order Data/Telephone Sys. Equipment	Y	Nynex delays	30d	3d	TS	4/25/96
52	Order Security Equipment			30d	3d	TS	6/6/96
53	**Perform Sitework**			15d	123.25d	TS	2/15/96
54	Identify Utilities	Y	No resources	5d	16.25d	?,?	2/15/96
55	Excavate Site			10d	31d	LAB,PM	2/15/96
56	Build Foundation			15d	76d	LAB,PM	2/15/96

and there was a lot to worry about. The scope of the project is evident from the following raw statistics:

- 37,500 official entrants, 20,000 bandits (illegal runners) expected
- 200,000 attendees expected at the Expo
- 840 buses to take runners from Copley Square to the Hopkinton starting point
- 2,300 medical personnel
- 1,500,000 spectators along the way
- 120,000,000 households worldwide T.V. audience
- 80 race officials
- 190 massage therapists, 122 physical therapists
- 600 state police, 60 motorcycle police
- 1,500 members of the press
- 90,000+ applications mailed, 33,000 rejected

Consider the marathon course. It involves:

- 36 course clocks, 14 checkpoints
- 72 mile marker signs, 26 Red Cross stations
- 24 YMCA water stations; 80 volunteers at each water station
- Extensive quantities of food to be obtained and served
- Extensive quantities of medical supplies/equipment to be used
- Race-related equipment to be ordered, installed, and used

There were Boston Marathon T-shirts and hats, a website on the Internet, and even a Boston Marathon wine. Five hundred cases of red wine and 750 cases of white wine, complete with commemorative 100th Boston Marathon labels, were made. Traffic movement was going to be a problem. The I-495 ramp into Hopkinton was to be closed after 6 A.M., as were all other roads into town.

Like a typical project, risks came out of nowhere. Race Director Guy Morse had invited President Clinton, who enjoyed running and marathons, to watch the race. The last Morse heard, Clinton couldn't attend, though rumors said otherwise.

If Clinton had decided to come, it would have made Morse's logistical nightmare even worse. Not only would he have had to handle 39,000 official runners, several thousand "bandit runners," and a million spectators, he would also have had to deal with the Secret Service and the added security measures.

Dave McGillivray, the race's technical coordinator for the past nine years, deliberately tortured himself before the race this year. He had to plan for everything. "I would sit there and play the 'What if?' game," he told a reporter for the *Hartford Courant* before the 1996 race. "What if there are 50,000 bandits? What if I can't fit the people into the athletes' village in Hopkinton? What if it snows?"

Call him paranoid, but McGillivray had developed contingency plans for every situation. An emergency on the course? It's never happened before, but the marathon can be rerouted if it does.

"It seems like a lot of work and planning for something that might not happen," McGillivray told the *Courant*, "But we have to do it." Recall that the investment in risk management is two to four percent, but the consequences would be disastrous if something happens at run time!

McGillivray was almost done and he was planning to travel from Boston to Hopkinton, hop on to Route 135, and run the marathon. "I am looking forward to doing it myself," he told the *Courant*.

A good project manager should be as relaxed as McGillivray! He put a substantial effort into project risk management. He identified key risks, quantified the high risks, mitigated them, and implemented a contingency plan for the highest risks. The 100th Boston Marathon was going to be a success.

TEST YOURSELF

1. Has risk management been accepted in your organization? If so, what is the methodology being used to practice project risk management?

2. Consider your last project that you worked on. List three risks that you experienced in this project. How did you mitigate the risks?

3. For the Boston Marathon case study, identify at least five risks. Put them in the template shown in figure 10.5 below.

4. Create a risk response strategy for any three of the five risks that you have identified. Complete the table shown in figure 10.8 below.

5. Implement contingency plans for any three risks. Complete the template shown in figure 10.9.

Figure 10.8 Risk Response Planning Template

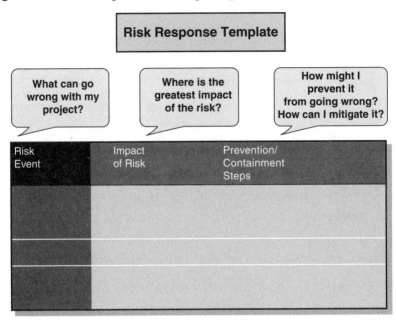

Figure 10.9 Risk Contingency Planning Template

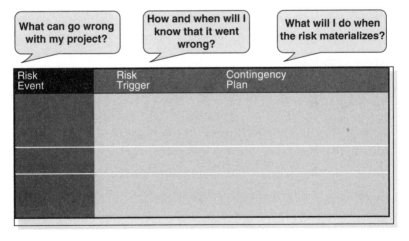

KEY POINTS TO REMEMBER

- Risks are present in all projects, big and small. While the project manager will play a key role, risk management is a shared responsibility of all project team members.

- Risk management is recognized as a best practice in project management for reducing the surprise factor.

- The key strategy with risk management is "prevention is better than the cure."

- Pure risks deal with a loss, one that can be deflected or transferred to another party through a contract or insurance policy. There are no opportunities associated with a pure risk, only losses.

- Business risks can result in profit and must be maximized.

- The risk management plan is part of the project plan.

- The risk management plan identifies risks, defines them, mitigates them, and provides a framework to monitor and control them throughout the project.

- The purpose of the risk identification process is to identify all risks that may impact the project, document them, and identify their characteristics.

- Qualitative risk analysis ranks risks by their impact and probability of occurrence.

- Quantitative risk analysis evaluates the impacts of risk prioritized during the qualitative risk analysis process and quantifies risk exposure for the project by assigning numeric probabilities to each risk and its impact on project objectives.

- Risk response planning is the process where risk response plans are developed using strategies such as avoidance, transference, mitigation, acceptance, and sharing.

- Project risk monitoring and control is a key step—it includes communicating risks to stakeholders and to senior management.

- Risk management is an iterative process.

- You cannot identify and mitigate all risks in a project, so focus on three to five risks and mitigate them completely for most small projects. For larger projects, identify ten key risks that you must mitigate fully. This is called top-down risk management.

- Once your WBS is created, identify activities that are high risks and flag them for closer monitoring and control. This is called bottom-up risk management.

Project Quality Management

INTRODUCTION

Quality management is a key knowledge area of project management. In today's market-driven, competitive society, quality is essential. Customers demand it, stakeholders expect it, and project teams know that their project will be regarded as a failure if the quality objectives are not achieved. Achieving time and cost objectives will mean nothing to your stakeholders if they are not happy with the quality.

WHAT'S AHEAD

- What is quality
- Quality management
  - Understand quality management
  - Define quality and related key words
  - Cost of quality
- Developing a quality management plan
- Understanding the three steps in project quality
  - Quality planning
  - Quality assurance
  - Quality control
- Overview of key quality control tools

IN THE REAL WORLD

A review of the Toyota recalls for some 2007 year models reveals the following defect information:

- Toyota Camry: air bags
- Toyota Tacoma: power train driveline
- Toyota Camry: side air bags
- Toyota Cruiser: tires
- Toyota Sequoia: brakes and hydraulic foundation

Even some of the power steering of the popular hybrid was defective. For one of the largest car manufacturers in the world and a company that has made its reputation on quality, this information is bad news. *Consumer Reports* now will no longer recommend any new or redesigned Toyota-built models without reliability data on the new design. Previously, *Consumer Reports* recommended Toyota models automatically because of the automaker's excellent track record, even if the publication didn't have sufficient reliability data on the new model. This policy will stand until Toyota returns to its previous record of outstanding overall quality and reliability.

Similar bad reports on Toyota defects from all over the world have shaken the company to its roots and even angered the Japanese government. Toyota has been asked by the government to explain the quality problems and list the steps they are going to take to resolve the issue. In response, Toyota has hired more engineers and has also assigned a second executive vice president to its quality control division. It has also created a new senior managing director position dedicated to improving quality. Since communication of defective parts and consumer complaints holds the key to quality assurance, Toyota has promised to create a new computer database to obtain information more quickly from dealers on repairs and complaints.

According to the *International Herald Tribune* (August 8, 2006), at Toyota's 2006 annual executive meeting in June, its outgoing chairman, Hiroshi Okuda, its new chairman, Fujio Cho, and its chief executive, Katsuaki Watanabe, all vowed to the gathered managers that the quality issue would be addressed. According to a senior Toyota executive who attended the meeting, "The quality issue is a big concern. They're embarrassed about it. You think about Toyota, and quality is in our DNA. We are concerned about looking like the rest of the pack. The market is forgiving because of our long reputation, but how long will they be forgiving?"

Meanwhile, the American automakers have realized that one of the key reasons they have lost market share to German and Japanese automakers is because of poor quality. Companies like Ford have put quality plans in place to fully meet quality expectations. They know their survival as a company depends on manufacturing reliable cars with excellent quality. Dr. Deming, the famous American statistician has stated many times that, "Americans still care about quality. The country is full of intelligent, courageous people who would change … if they only knew how important it was to improve quality and productivity." He believes that businesses attempting to compete in this global world must establish a quality-first culture, and empower employees to participate as entrepreneurs and to enlist their ideas in continuously improving products and services. Time will tell if American automobile companies like Ford will succeed in this competitive global world by anchoring on a quality-first strategy and if Toyota will get its quality reputation back.

KEY CONCEPTS

The above example explains the importance of quality. There is no debate about who is ultimately responsible for quality in an organization. It is the responsibility of senior management to create a quality-enabling environment. What actions must senior management take to ensure quality in the project management realm?

1. Publicly declare the philosophy and corporate commitment to quality.

2. Set the standards and provide resources to support excellence in quality management.

3. Implement organization-wide training in the concepts and principles involved.

4. Set up measurement programs to establish the current quality level.

5. Identify problem areas and look for solutions that will prevent problems from reappearing.

6. Monitor to see if the solutions are improving the quality levels.

7. Empower staff at all levels and get them involved with working in the quality environment.

It should also be clear that the project manager, as the senior representative of the organization, must have very high quality standards and create a quality-first environment. These ideals must be clearly communicated to project teams.

PROJECT QUALITY MANAGEMENT

What is quality? The International Organization for Standardization (ISO) defines quality as "the degree to which a set of inherent characteristics fulfills requirements." Unlike the terms *risk* or *cost*, which are easy to define, quality is difficult to define as it means different things to different people. To add to the complexity, the project manager has to be concerned with quality of project management in addition to quality of the product or service that is being produced. So for our purposes, we can define quality as both conformance to requirements and the ability of the project manager to deliver the requirements on schedule and within the allocated budget. This definition satisfactorily addresses quality from both the product perspective and the project management perspective. Both aspects are important.

We can define quality as:

a) Conformance to requirements

b) The ability of the project manager to deliver the requirements on schedule and within the allocated budget

---

Note the focus on project management processes. At the outset it may not be apparent why the customer should care about project management or the project manager's ability to deliver the requirements on time. But getting a project completed on budget and on time will result in a lower product price and will make the organization more competitive. Therefore, project quality is a key attribute in our definition of success.

WHAT IS QUALITY?

To understand quality let us look at examples, and first we'll consider the case of the construction industry. If a customer buys a house, quality to the customer implies meeting all building codes, using construction materials that will last for a long time, and having fixtures that work satisfactorily. The customer certainly does not want to see water coming in through the foundation or water leaking through the roof after a heavy rainfall.

Let us next look at an information technology example and investigate the purchase of the Microsoft Vista operating system—which is the subject of our case study in this book. You paid a steep price for the software, and spent a substantial amount of your time to install it. So you have a definition of quality. First and foremost, you would like to see the promised functionality. Is the new operating system capable of doing all that was promised? It gets tricky for some attributes. How would we define quality as it pertains to "shelf life"? Would you define it as follows?

A. "The vendor must support the software for a long time. I don't plan to switch to another operating system any time in the near future!"

Or would you define it as follows?

B. "I don't care if the product does not last forever. I know Microsoft will come up with a new operating system soon. They always do to support newer processors. I will abandon this software instantly when the new software arrives."

If you were manufacturing automobiles or electronics products, this dilemma is again apparent. Many customers lease a car or trade in frequently. They only care about reliability for five years or less. Others want to keep the car for a dozen years. The lesson learned here is that the project manager must uncover the customer's quality expectations up front and not after the project has begun. If the customer desires a product "of good quality," this must be measured and benchmarked to avoid miscommunication after the product has been delivered.

We can always measure quality using the following attributes—performance, reliability, flexibility, maintainability, and capability. It is the project manager's responsibility to discover the customer's expectations for these attributes.

For example, let us explore reliability and maintainability. Consider again the new Microsoft Vista operating system that the customer has purchased. The customer will want no fatal defects in the software. He or she will certainly not want to uninstall the software and go back to the previous operating system. That is a nightmare to even seasoned computer professionals!

This implies that the definition of quality from the customer's perspective is "no bugs in code—period." So when the software is being designed, it must work toward being "bug free" (reliability) or have a transparent process in place that will ensure that it is "bug free" (maintainability). The following table summarizes key measures for quality for a new operating system or software.

Table 11.1 Quality Attributes

Functionality	Capability and security
Usability	User friendly and good documentation or help
Reliability	"Bug free" or should be maintained transparently
Performance	Faster than the previous product
Supportability	Should be transparently maintained

Grade versus Quality

Grade and quality are frequently confused. Poor grade does not imply poor quality. Consider the case of the Toyota automobiles. One can regard the Toyota Camry as being in a different grade of quality when compared with the Toyota Lexus. The former is a good utility car and the latter a popular luxury car. They each serve a purpose, with different expectations. Or, if you are into gold and jewelry, 22 carat gold is higher grade than 14 carat gold. But people buy jewelry containing both grades of gold purity.

Price of Conformance

The price of conformance is the price we pay to ensure a quality product. This includes attributes such as training, inspection and defect removal, developing and implementing standards, and setting and running a quality measurement program. The price of conformance is the cost involved in making certain that things are done right the first time.

Price of Nonconformance

Since quality is conformance to requirements, then we should also be able to measure the quality of something by the degree to which it does not meet requirements. This is referred to as price of nonconformance. A measure of quality is therefore the degree of its nonconformance, which is anything that causes the product to fail. The lower the price of nonconformance, the higher will be the product quality. The price of nonconformance is the money wasted when work fails to conform to customer requirements.

Cost of Quality

The cost of quality refers to the total cost of all efforts incurred in producing the product. The total cost of quality is the sum of the price of conformance and the price of nonconformance. An organization can save money by cutting down on activities that pertain to the price of nonconformance. Examples include rework, scrap, warranty, customer support, product maintenance, and the product recall infrastructure. Managers are frequently reluctant to invest in quality because they conclude that rework and scrap are inevitably going to occur no matter how much is invested toward cost of conformance.

The cost of quality includes costs associated with carrying out quality-related processes. These costs can be categorized as follows:

- Prevention costs: Quality planning, technical reviews, testing equipment, training
- Appraisal costs: Inspection and testing
- Failure costs: Internal—rework; external—technical support, customer support

RISK MANAGEMENT PROCESS

According to the PMBOK, project quality management includes the following three processes:

1. Quality planning: Identifying which quality standards are relevant to the project and determining how to satisfy them

Figure 11.1 Quality Management Processes

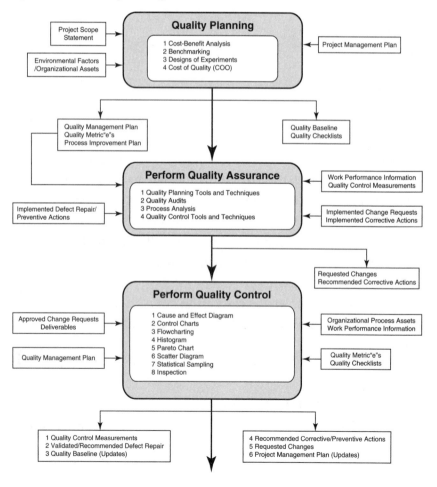

2. Quality assurance: Applying the planned, systematic quality activities to ensure that the project employs all processes needed to meet requirements

3. Quality control: Monitoring specific project results to determine whether they comply with relevant quality standards and identifying ways to eliminate causes of unsatisfactory performance

Quality Planning

Quality planning is an important step. A common principle of quality management is that "quality is planned in, not inspected in." In other words, we should not expect quality to mysteriously appear at the end of the project. The goal is to capture defects early. The 1:10:100 rule of thumb clearly lays a case for this goal. This rule states that the cost and effort to fix defects increases ten times from the requirements phase to the post-design phase, and another tenfold from the design phase to the implementation phase.

Quality planning answers the following questions:

• What quality standards are relevant to the project?

• How will these standards be satisfied?

Like many other project management processes, it is necessary to perform quality planning throughout the project life cycle. It may be necessary to make product changes to meet identified quality standards. A key input to quality planning is the organization's quality policy. If a quality policy does not exist, the project manager must develop and document one for the project.

The scope statement must also be considered as a primary input during the quality planning stage, as the customer's expectations for quality might be clearly documented there. The project objectives and narrative of the deliverables should be considered in creating a quality policy.

While planning for quality standards and regulations requires special consideration, compliance to certain codes is mandatory and the project manager must be knowledgeable about industry-specific standards.

There is a difference between a standard and a regulation. A standard is a document approved by a recognized body. A regulation is a document that lays down specifications and characteristics for which compliance is mandatory.

The following tools and techniques play key roles in quality planning:

- Cost/benefit analysis: The benefits must outweigh the costs when producing a product in the short term or in the long term, whichever if that is the strategy of the organization.

- Benchmarking: The best measurable performance for a metric is identified. Project managers can look at other organizations for the best performance on that metric.

- Flowcharting: Flowcharts are used as quality planning tools to identify problems in project processes, make a project process visible, standardize processes, create a picture of an ideal process, support organizational learning and document processes that work. (See Figure 11.2).

- Fishbone diagrams: These are also known as Ishikawa diagrams, and they help analyze a process to identify the possible causes of errors. The head of the fish is the defect, and the inputs to the process are the bones of the fish. (See Figure 11.3).

Figure 11.2 Flowchart Example

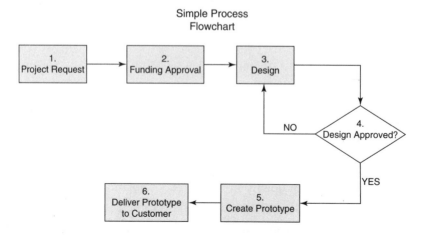

Figure 11.3 Example of a Fishbone Diagram

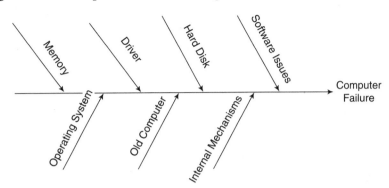

Quality Management Plan

One of the key outputs of quality planning is the quality management plan. The PMBOK guide defines the quality management plan as follows:

> The quality management plan describes the methods by which the project team implements the performing organization's quality policy. The quality management plan is a component of the project management plan and must address quality control (QC), quality assurance (QA), and continuous process improvement for the project. The quality management plan may be formal or informal, highly detailed or broadly framed, based on the requirements of the project.

This plan describes the project's quality management system to the project stakeholders. It addresses the following issues:

- Scope of the quality management system
- Involvement of external quality-based groups and enforcement of standards
- Identifies the quality standards that must be met
- Identifies the approaches, tools, and techniques that will be employed

- Quality control: tracking and reporting defects and discrepancies
- Validation of each deliverable

Quality Assurance

Quality assurance is simply defined as the process of evaluating overall project performance on a regular basis to provide confidence that the project will satisfy the relevant quality standards. A quality assurance department, or similar organization, often oversees quality assurance activities. QA support, regardless of the unit's title, may be provided to the project team, the management of the performing organization, the customer or sponsor, as well as other stakeholders. Quality assurance assures us that the project delivers appropriate levels of quality. Quality assurance also supports continuous process improvement. In the software industry, quality assurance involves activities such as reviews, inspections, and testing.

The key inputs for quality assurance are the quality management plan and results of quality control measurements. The key tools for this process are quality audits, which examine the effectiveness of quality activities. An audit will identify key recommendations that can improve the performance of a project.

A key output of the quality assurance process is quality improvement of the project, which depends on continuous quality control and adjustment.

Quality Control

The PMBOK guide defines quality control as follows:

> The process of monitoring specific project results to determine whether they comply with relevant quality standards and identifying ways to eliminate causes of unsatisfactory results. It should be performed throughout the project. The project management team should have a working knowledge of statistical quality control, especially sampling and probability, to help evaluate quality control outputs. The main outputs from quality control are quality control status reports, performance data, rework, process improvements, acceptance decisions, and completed checklists.

The project results monitored by quality control include results such as cost and schedule variances. Variances are important as they represent deviations from the plan. A variety of tools and methods are used for performing quality control. Some of them are introduced in the next topic.

Quality Control Tools

We will review the following quality control tools: management reviews, walk-throughs and inspections, control charts, and Pareto analysis.

Management Reviews, Walk-Throughs, and Inspections

Product quality data must only be obtained from direct examination of the work or product itself. This examination must be conducted by the project manager, by a team member acting as the manager's representative, or by an impartial evaluator. Preferably, work products should be examined by a technical expert who is not a member of the team. In this way, product quality is objectively evaluated.

In the software industry, one way to examine the quality of work products is by conducting a formal, structured walk-through. Another way to evaluate product quality is to review the product documentation which is often a good indicator of product quality and will help determine if requirements have been met.

Data to be evaluated can be divided into performance data and criteria data, some examples of which are listed below:

Quality: Performance Data

- Well-defined tasks with tangible end products
- Forms to document work products
- Procedures for quality reviews at milestones

Quality: Criteria Data

- Standards, including sample work products
- Procedures for bringing expertise to quality reviews

Control Chart

A control chart reveals whether or not a process is stable or has predictable performance. A control chart is a data gathering tool which serves to show when a process is subject to a special cause variation. When a variation occurs, it shows in the control chart as data which is out of bounds and which indicates an out-of-control condition.

Control charts are useful as they display graphically how a process behaves over time. See figure 11.4. Control limits are the lines that are two or three standard deviations on either side of the centerline, or mean, of a normal distribution. Data plotted on a control chart should reflect the expected variation in the data. When a measurement is outside the control limits, it should be investigated to determine the cause of the condition.

Ideally, the data samples should randomly appear on both sides of the mean. One rule of thumb is called the Rule of Seven. This rule states that if seven or more observations in a row occur on the same side of the mean or if they trend in the same direction—even though they may be within the control limits—they should be investigated as though they had an assignable cause.

Note that in figure 11.5 the samples to the left of the average are all between the average and the upper control limit (UCL). Even though the data points are within the control limits, they are all on the same side of the mean. This implies that the process is out of control. It is possible that wear and tear in the equipment is taking place.

Also note the lone sample on the right side that is out of control, as it appears above the upper control limit. This process should be investigated further.

Figure 11.4 Sample Control Chart

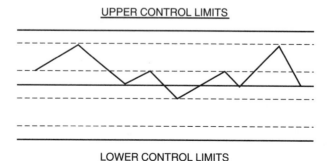

UPPER CONTROL LIMITS

LOWER CONTROL LIMITS

Figure 11.5 Control Chart with "Out of Control" Data Points

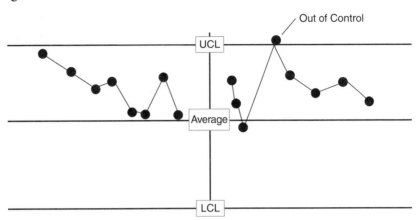

Pareto Analysis

Pareto's Law says that a relatively small number of causes will typically produce a large majority of the problems or defects. Although not really a law, it is a useful rule of thumb named after the 19th century Italian economist Vilfredo Pareto, who observed that 80 percent of the income in Italy went to 20 percent of the population.

A Pareto chart or diagram is used in order to select the most important problem areas of the project. Using the Pareto idea, the most important problems will cause the most trouble. That is, 20 percent of the problems are responsible for 80 percent of the total cost of the project's problems.

Six Sigma

We cannot conclude our discussion on quality control without introducing the concept of Six Sigma. Six Sigma is a measure of quality or near perfection originally developed by Motorola to improve processes by eliminating defects. Six Sigma is a combination of philosophy and tools aimed at quality improvement. It has the Plan-Do-Check-Act cycle and the following principles at its core:

- Processes can be analyzed, measured, and controlled.
- Continuous effort must be exerted to reduce process variations and to improve quality.
- Continuous success requires top management commitment.

Many companies use Six Sigma methodologies for improvements, ranging from manufacturing to inventory management and design. Process engineering and business process improvement are also closely tied with Six Sigma strategies. Processes that operate with Six Sigma quality expect to generate less than 3.4 defects per million opportunities. Organizations striving for such high standards are disciplined, apply a data-driven approach, and have a process in place to eliminate defects.

QUALITY IN ACTION

The Big Dig project was planned, designed, and constructed over a period of 24 years from 1983 through 2007. Preliminary design started in the mid 1980s and final design began in the late 1980s. The project began construction in late 1991, and in the same year the Supplemental Environmental Impact Statement was approved.

Because of the technological and environmental challenges of the Big Dig project, maintaining quality was a key focus of project management throughout the construction. Early on, a quality assurance (QA) program was established and quality control became a key focus of the executive management team.

As part of the Big Dig project's quality assurance program, the project's joint venture manager performed quality assurance checks of the contractor's work for general compliance with contractual requirements and approved submittals, as well as with each contractor's quality assurance program. Responsibility for control of quality belonged to the contractor in accordance with the contract, regulations and guidelines, and general industry practice.

However, the section design consultants (SDCs) on each contract remained actively engaged throughout the construction phase, as the engineers of record. As appropriate, the project manager facilitated the resolution of issues between or among contractors, section design consultants, and the state. In addition, significant issues and challenges that arose during the design and construction of the Big Dig project were typically brought to the attention of the project interface committee, comprised of state and federal government representatives and senior project managers.

In 2003, the state assumed responsibility for operations, inspections, and maintenance of the completed portion of the tunnels and roadway. Quality assurance remained a major issue through project completion, and the Big Dig continues to require extensive monitoring through the operational stage.

TEST YOURSELF

1. Has a quality-first culture been accepted in your organization? If so, what steps have been taken? Why do you believe that your organization is committed to quality?

2. You have been asked to lead your team to deliver a quality project on time and under budget. Due to changes in project scope, you have to consider sacrificing schedule, cost, or quality. Assuming that you don't want to sacrifice quality, what steps will you take next?

3. You are asked to create a project quality definition table for a) a software development project (a database-driven website) or b) a construction industry project (a house). Complete five quality items for the following quality definition table. We have shown you one example.

Quality Item	Measurable Item	Unit of Measure
Reliability: Zero defects and stable software	• Error reports • Downtime	• Mean time between failures • % Downtime < 1%

4. Create a complete quality plan for the above project. Once again, you can choose between either a) a software development project (a database-driven website) or b) a construction industry project (a house).

KEY POINTS TO REMEMBER

- We can define quality as conformance to requirements and the ability of the project manager to deliver the requirements on time and schedule and within the allocated budget.
- The project manager has ultimate responsibility for the project quality.
- Exceeding customer expectations is called gold-plating and may introduce risks to the project. Conformance to requirements is a more important strategy.
- Examples of the costs of conformance: planning; training and indoctrination; process control; product design validation; process validation; tests and evaluations; quality audits; maintenance and calibration; inspection and field-testing.
- Examples of the costs of nonconformance: scrap; rework and repair; additional material or inventory; warranty repairs and service; complaint handling; liability judgments; product recalls; field service; expediting. The costs of prevention and conformance are less than the costs of quality defects, so we must invest in costs of prevention.
- Grade and quality should not be confused. A product could have a lower grade, as it may have unique functional use; it must still have good quality.
- The organization is responsible for setting quality standards and showing leadership in this regard.
- The cost of quality falls into three categories: prevention costs, appraisal costs, and failure costs.
- The 1:10:100 rule of thumb states that the cost and effort to fix defects increases ten times from the requirements phase to the post-design phase and another tenfold from the design phase to the implementation phase.
- The following tools for quality management form a basis for an overall methodology: flowchart, the cause-and-effect (fishbone or Ishikawa) diagram, the Pareto diagram, the check sheet, the scatter diagram, the histogram, and the control chart.

Advanced Project Planning

INTRODUCTION

The job of the project manager is to manage the performance, cost, and schedule of the project. In this chapter, we focus on determining the *true* cost and schedule of the project. What will the project really cost? Is the project actually on schedule?

IN THE REAL WORLD

You're the project manager and you sidle up to one of your workers and ask,

"How ya doin'?"

"I'm about 50 percent done," he replies.

One week later, you try again.

"How ya doin'?"

"I'm about 50 percent done."

"But you were 50 percent done last week!"

"Yup, and I'm still about 50 percent done."

How do we get out of this trap? Earned value!

There is, in fact, a quite simple way to estimate the future final cost when we are in the middle of the project. We can also measure whether the project is on schedule.

WHAT'S AHEAD

- How to determine the true status of a project through deliverables
- Calculating:
  - Planned value (PV)
  - Actual cost (AC)
  - Earned value (EV)
- Measuring project performance through:
  - Cost performance index (CPI)
  - Schedule performance index (SPI)

KEY CONCEPTS

EARNED VALUE

The first question to be asked is, "What is the *value* of the work accomplished to date?" All of the following questions are directly pertinent:

What does it mean to be 50 percent done?

How do we give partial credit?

Should we give partial credit at all?

Take a look at figure 12.1. This is the sort of chart that is often shown to managers in an attempt to communicate project status. From the chart, it looks as if things are going well because the actual costs are running below the planned expenditures. The really important question is, "Is this project running ahead of schedule and under budget?"

Actually, from just this chart, you can't tell anything at all about the project's status. Let's examine why not.

The project began in January and there were supposed to be monthly deliverables. Figure 12.1 shows we are at the end of March (week 12) and so we should have completed three deliverables, which are indicated by the

Figure 12.1 Planned vs. Actual Costs

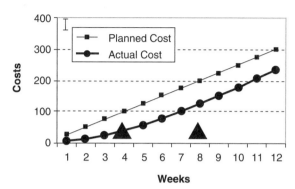

triangles (one each for January, February, and March). If the deliverables had been successfully completed, then maybe we would be ahead of our cost projections, since we are running under budget and would have delivered the required work for this stage of the project.

However, it appears that we have not completed the third deliverable, due at the end of week 12. Therefore, we cannot say whether we are running under cost or not. We may need to spend a lot of money to complete the unfinished deliverable. How do we resolve this dilemma?

This is known as the Work in Process Measurement Problem. It is a neglected issue, but also a great opportunity. Hopefully, by the end of this chapter, you will see that it is not difficult to make some real progress on this topic.

The first thing we need is an unambiguous, objective assessment of the work accomplished. How do we do that?

Only measurable deliverables reflect the true status of a project.

The only thing that counts is a completed deliverable. In simplistic terms, either you have delivered the promised item or you haven't. Not only that, you only get credit for a completed deliverable; "50 percent done" doesn't cut it.

Let's reconsider figure 12.1 and ask which of the deliverables have been completed. There were three deliverables scheduled by the end of March.

How many were completed? Two deliverables were actually finished, and that is very specific: two-thirds of the work has been completed.

Notice that we have gone from a vague observation about running under cost to a specific and meaningful measurement of progress. The project manager's assignment is now clear: investigate the missing deliverable. Is it in process? Does it need an extension? The important lesson is that the only way to track the actual progress is to monitor the deliverables. Anything else is just fuzzy, unquantifiable opinion.

The second lesson is that the measurement of the deliverables must be quantitative. There are many ways to measure deliverables. For example:

- Laying turf, measured in square yards per day
- Painting a room, measured in square meters of paint applied
- Writing a document, measured in completed sections or chapters
- Developing software, measured in debugged modules or lines of code
- Erecting steel, measured in number of girders installed

We have neglected the discussion of quality, which is a separate issue. Obviously, just delivering is not enough. Most deliverables go through some sort of review or quality control process. If the deliverable is judged to have acceptable quality, then at that point we can assume it is complete.

As the project manager facing the data in figure 12.1, you have *earned* the value of the two deliverables that were completed. Since the *planned* (or budgeted) work for this point in time was three deliverables, you should report that you have *earned* 66 percent of the work at this point.

Now we'll add the cost and schedule data. Suppose each deliverable is projected to cost $100, i.e., the planned cost for each deliverable is $100. At the end of March, you should have spent $300 and so the planned value of the deliverables is $300. According to figure 12.1, you have spent $250. This is the actual cost.

The complication is that you have not earned $300 worth of work, you have only earned $200 worth of work (two-thirds of the work, because two out of the three deliverables have been completed). Therefore, the earned value of the work actually accomplished is $200. So you have not delivered the work that you should have at this point. Even though you have only spent $250 and the plan was to spend $300, you have only accomplished $200 worth of work by spending $250.

You are over budget and behind schedule!

Now you see how deceptive figure 12.1 is. You may think that you are underrunning your budget. However, when you measure progress through the earned value of the deliverables, you get a true picture of the status of your project. Later on, we will add some fairly simple formulas to understand how far over budget and over schedule you are. But for now, you should understand the basic idea: The way to measure progress is to measure the *completed* deliverables. No deliverables, no progress.

We now see one of the key ideas behind decomposing the WBS into small, measurable activities with specific deliverables as outcomes. When the deliverable is complete, the value of its work is earned. The challenge for the project manager is to find a way to *measure* the progress of the deliverables. No more "50 percent done." One of the reasons for dividing activities into small units (one to two people for one to two weeks) is that it helps create and define measurable deliverables.

The earned value process is as follows:

- Identify short activities.
- Define a quantifiable measure of progress for each activity.
- Assign a schedule to each activity.
- Assign an effort to each activity.
- Measure the progress of each activity.
- You earn the earned value when the activity is complete.

Here's the important result:

> You earn the value
> of the work accomplished
> when the deliverable is complete.

PAINT MY GARAGE

To see how the process works in detail, we will follow a project to paint my garage. I hire a contractor, and he says that it should take four painters four days to do the job. He pays the painters $250 per day, so that is four painters × four days × $250 = $4,000 for the labor. The contractor estimates he'll need $1,000 worth of materials, so the total bid is $5,000.

Since painting my garage will be a major disruption, I decide to go away on vacation while the contractor does the work. The contractor starts on Monday and so that evening, I call to see how he is doing. He tells me that everything is fine and that his crew worked all day. I call at the end of each day, and I get the same report: the crew showed up, worked all day, and he paid them for their work.

I return on Friday morning to discover that they are not finished! What happened? The contractor says that they worked each day as planned. "If so," I ask, "why aren't you finished?" It turns out that they ran into a problem on Wednesday, because painting one of the windows was more difficult than they planned and took longer than they expected. Why didn't they report it? Because they had no way to measure progress! The contractor just assumed that it would all work out in the end.

The Earned Value Approach to the Painting of My Garage

If we had known about earned value, then we could have set up a much smarter way to manage the project. The first change is to make a detailed cost estimate, or bid, which is shown in figure 12.3.

Figure 12.2 Bid for the Garage Plant Job

- Technical Specifications:
  - Paint garage with four walls
  - Each wall is 20 ft × 10 ft, 200 square feet total for each wall
- Schedule:
  - Four days
- Cost:
  - Four people at $250 each for four days: $4,000
  - Materials: $1,000
    - Total Planned Cost: $5,000

Notice immediately that we have provided a measurable deliverable for the paint job. We divided the project into walls, and defined the area of each. Now we can measure the area painted each day. That is, we now have a quantifiable measure of progress: square feet painted per day.

The next step concerns the materials. The earned value rule for materials is "until you use it, I'm not paying for it." So rather than present the cost of the materials as $1,000 to be paid up front, the earned value process assigns value only as materials are used. In the case of my garage, that means that the value of the materials should be assigned as $250 per day.

Now we are ready to plan for Monday, day 1. The most important addition is that we have defined a quantitative measure for the activity for the day. We identify the area to be painted as 200 square feet. We will quantify the progress on the deliverable at the end of Monday by measuring the area that has been painted. Next, we assign the materials, $250 worth of paint, so the total planned value for Monday is $1,250. See figure 12.3. We then make a similar chart for Tuesday, Wednesday, and Thursday.

Figure 12.3 Detailed Planning for Monday

Activity	Schedule	Planned Value
Paint West Wall		
20'x10' = 200 sq ft	8 hrs	$1,000
Materials		$250
Total Planned Value:		**$1,250**

Figure 12.4 Earned Value for Day #1

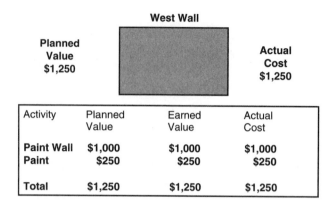

West Wall

| Planned Value $1,250 | | | | Actual Cost $1,250 |

Activity	Planned Value	Earned Value	Actual Cost
Paint Wall	$1,000	$1,000	$1,000
Paint	$250	$250	$250
Total	$1,250	$1,250	$1,250

Figure 12.5 Earned Value for Day #3

South Wall

| Planned Value $1,250 | | | | Actual Cost $1,250 |

Activities	Planned Value	Earned Value	Actual Cost
Paint Wall	$1,000	$500	$1,000
Paint	$250	$250	$250
Total	$1,250	$750	$1,250

Confident that I have a good plan, I can now go on vacation and let the contractor paint my garage. On Monday, I call and ask how things went. The contractor says that they worked all day as planned.

But now I am a lot smarter, and I ask, "How many square feet did you paint today?" The contractor, somewhat taken aback by this request, says he painted the entire west wall, all 200 square feet. I fill out my earned value chart, Figure 12.4.

The actual cost was $1,000 worth of labor and $250 worth of materials, for a total actual cost of $1,250. I measure the work performed, which is 200 square feet of wall. The value of the work performed is my earned value, which is $1,000 worth of labor and $250 worth of materials. So on Monday my earned value is equal to my actual cost. The project is on schedule and on budget.

On Tuesday, evening, I call again and the contractor tells me he has completed the painting of the north wall. Not to be put off, I again ask, "How many square feet did you paint today?" The contractor, slightly annoyed by my request, says he painted the entire north wall, all 200 square feet. I thank him for his patience, and fill out my earned value chart. Tuesday's earned value chart will look exactly the same as Monday's. My project is still on schedule and on budget.

On Wednesday evening, I call and the contractor tells me that they ran into a problem with the south wall. When they moved some of my junk in the garage, they discovered a window, and the window needed a lot of extra work. I ask how many square feet they completed. The contractor, somewhat reluctantly, tells me that they painted half of the wall, only 100 square feet. I fill out my earned value chart for Wednesday, figure 12.5.

The planned value is the same as Monday and Tuesday. The contractor purchased the paint, so the cost for that is $250. The contractor's crew worked all day Wednesday, so they are entitled to their pay, $1,000. Therefore, the total actual cost is $1,250. Unfortunately, they ran into the window problem, so they did not earn the value that was scheduled for Wednesday.

When I assess the progress for Wednesday, I can actually measure that they only painted 100 square feet. This is the important point about defining measurable deliverables. If I had not established that I expect 200 square feet of painting per day, I would have no way of measuring the actual progress. Since the painters completed only half of the wall, they earn only 50 percent of the work for Wednesday. Therefore, the earned value for the labor on Wednesday is only $500. Since the purchase of the paint was a legitimate cost, the earned value for the paint is $250. The total earned value for Wednesday is $750.

As a smart project manager, I immediately ask him about options for finishing the project. He proposes to finish the job on Friday morning. Because he knows he will have to paint the remaining 100 square feet of wall on Friday, he estimates that the additional cost will be half a day's work, or $500.

I ask the contractor if it is possible to finish the job on time. He thinks about it for a few minutes and says that there are two options: he can try to find another painter by tomorrow, or use the existing crew and work overtime. He thinks it is unlikely that he can find another painter by tomorrow morning, so the only realistic option is to use overtime. He explains that overtime will add even more to the cost.

I decide not to pay for overtime and ask the contractor to finish up on Friday morning. I agree to pay the extra $500.

This is project management at its best. When a problem is discovered, the parties immediately sit down and analyze options. Technical problems, exceptions, and changes are a fact of life for a project manager, and the sooner that they are dealt with, the more options there are to deal with them.

On Thursday, the plan is for the contractor to paint the east wall. I call Thursday evening and learn that they finished the half of the south wall left over from Wednesday and painted half of the east wall. Their earned value chart is similar to Monday's, in that they were scheduled to paint 200 square feet and did so. They also purchased $250 worth of paint, as scheduled. Unfortunately, because of the window problem on Tuesday, they did not finish the east wall, so they are still behind by 100 square feet. They were scheduled to finish the job on Thursday, so they have not completed the job—they will need to come back on Friday to finish.

On Friday, they paint the half of the east wall they did not finish on Thursday. It does indeed take them half a day to finish the wall, so the cost for half a wall (100 square feet) is $500. This is the amount of the overrun for the project.

One of the constants of project management is change. All projects run into unexpected problems, and a project manager must be prepared to deal with them. Earned value tells the project manager precisely how big the problem is.

In my garage example, I know on Wednesday evening that I have a problem. The window problem was unforeseen, and the contractor's approach is quite reasonable, so there is little point in getting mad at the contractor. I only discovered the issue by insisting on measuring the contractor's progress in terms of square feet of paint.

Notice the difference when earned value is used. I agreed to pay the extra and accepted that the job will finish on Friday. I was a party to the agreement. Without the earned value approach, I would arrive home on Friday to find the job unfinished and a bill for another $500. I would be both surprised and mad.

CALCULATING EARNED VALUE

We now show how to use earned value to track scheduled progress and to estimate the final cost of the project. The planned value is the schedule of work as a function of time and is computed cumulatively as the project evolves.

Planned Value, PV

The time-phased baseline of the value of the work scheduled

The earned value is the percent of the planned budget that has been *earned* by actual work completed.

Earned Value, EV

The percent complete times the activity's planned budget

The actual cost is simply the total of all costs incurred to date.

Actual Cost, AC

The sum of the costs incurred accomplishing the work

To measure the deviation between the planned and actual progress from a cost perspective, we define two quantities that allow us to quantify the progress of our expenditures: the cost variance, CV, and the cost performance index, CPI.

Cost Variance, CV

The difference between the earned value and the actual costs
for the work completed to date:

$$CV = EV - AC$$

Cost Performance Index, CPI

The ratio of earned value to actual cost:

$$CPI = \frac{EV}{AC}$$

To measure the deviation between the planned and actual progress in the schedule, we define two quantities: the schedule variance, SV, and the schedule performance index, SPI.

Schedule Variance, SV

The difference between the earned value and the planned value
for the work completed to date

$$SV = EV - PV$$

Schedule Performance Index, SPI

The ratio of earned value to planned value

$$SPI = \frac{EV}{PV}$$

Cost Variance (CV) and Cost Performance Index (CPI)

Table 12.1 presents the cost performance parameters for the garage painting project. The planned values are shown in column 2, the actual costs in column 3, and the cumulative actual costs in column 4. On the first four days, the actual costs are $1,000 for the labor and $250 for the paint. On day five, the painters finish up and the actual labor cost is $500.

Table 12.1 Cost Variance (CV) and Cost Performance Index (CPI) for the Garage Project

Day	Planned Value	Actual Cost	Cumulative Actual Cost (AC)	Earned Value	Cumulative Earned Value (EV)	Cost Variance (CV=EV–AC)	CPI
1	$1,250	$1,250	$1,250	$1,250	$1,250	0	1.000
2	$1,250	$1,250	$2,500	$1,250	$2,500	0	1.000
3	$1,250	$1,250	$3,750	$750	$3,250	–$500	0.867
4	$1,250	$1,250	$5,000	$1,250	$4,500	–$500	0.900
5	0	$500	$5,500	$500	$5,000	–$500	0.909

The earned value on Monday and Tuesday is the same as the actual costs, since all of the planned work was completed. However, the earned value for the labor on Wednesday is $500, because the painters only completed half of the wall. The total earned value for day three is $500 for the labor, and $250 for the paint. The earned value on day 4 is the same as the actual costs, since $1,000 worth of work was completed along with $250 worth of paint. Finally, on day 5, the last $500 worth of work was earned as the job was finished up. The cumulative earned value is shown in column 6.

The cost variance is the *cumulative* earned value (EV) minus the *cumulative* actual cost (AC): CV = EV – AC. For days 1 and 2, the earned value is the same as the actual cost, so the cost variance, CV = 0. On day 3, the earned value for the labor is only $500, which when added to the earned value of the paint ($250) results in a cumulative earned value of $3,250 ($1,250 + $1,250 + $750 = $3,250). The cumulative actual costs are $3,750 ($1,250 + $1,250 + $1,250 = $3,750), so the cost variance for day 3 is CV = EV – AC = $ 3,250 – $3,750 = –$500. The cost variance is negative, indicating that the project is running over budget. Negative cost variances are bad, positive cost variances are good.

The cost performance index is the ratio of the earned value to the actual cost, CPI = EV/AC = $3,250/$3750 = 0.866. When the CPI is less than one, the project is running over budget. The CPI is more useful than the CV because it measures the overrun as a ratio, rather than as a number. A CV of $1,000 might mean a CPI of either 0.99 or 0.75. A CPI of 0.99 is not a value for concern, whereas a CPI of 0.75 represents a big problem.

Schedule Variance (SV) and Schedule Performance Index (SPI)

Table 12.2 presents the schedule performance parameters for the garage painting project. The planned values are shown in column 2 and the cumulative planned values in column 3. The earned values are shown in column 4 and the cumulative earned values in column 5. The earned values are the same as in table 12.1.

The schedule variance is the difference between the *cumulative* earned value and the *cumulative* planned value: $SV = EV - PV$. The schedule variance is shown in column 6. The schedule variance turns negative on day 3. Since the schedule variance is negative, the project is running behind schedule. Negative schedule variances are bad, positive schedule variances are good.

The schedule performance index is the ratio of the earned value to the planned value, $SPI = EV/PV$. For day 3, $SPI = \$3,250/\$3750 = 0.866$. When the SPI is less than one, the project is running behind schedule. The SPI is more useful than the SV because it measures the overrun as a ratio, rather than as a number. An SV of $1,000 might mean an SPI of either 0.99 or 0.75. An SPI of 0.99 is not a value for concern, whereas an SPI of 0.75 represents a big problem.

For the garage project, on day 3, the CPI falls below 1.0 and remains there for the duration of the project. This is quite characteristic of projects.

Table 12.2 Schedule Variance (SV) and Schedule Performance Index (SPI) for the Garage Project

Day	Planned Value	Cumulative Planned Value (PV)	Earned Value	Cumulative Earned Value (EV)	Schedule Variance (SV=EV–PV)	SPI
1	$1,250	$1,250	$1,250	$1,250	0	1.000
2	$1,250	$2,500	$1,250	$2,500	0	1.000
3	$1,250	$3,750	$750	$3,250	–$500	0.867
4	$1,250	$5,000	$1,250	$4,500	–$500	0.900
5	0	$5,000	$500	$5,000	0	1.000

Once they become late, they stay late. The behavior of the SPI is a little different. The SPI always approaches 1.0 at the end of the project because all of the work to be performed eventually gets completed. Therefore, the cumulative earned value always eventually catches up with the cumulative planned value. This is shown in table 12.2, where on day 5, the work is finally complete resulting in an SPI of 1.0.

Figures 12.6 through 12.11 show the cost and schedule parameters for the garage painting project as a function of time. Figure 12.6 shows the earned value falling behind the planned value, but eventually catching up on day 5. Figure 12.7 shows the earned value and actual cost. The actual cost increases on day 3 (because of the window problem) and stays ahead of the planned value for the remainder of the project.

Figure 12.6 Earned Value and Planned Value

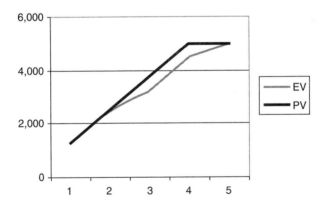

Figure 12.7 Earned Value and Actual Cost

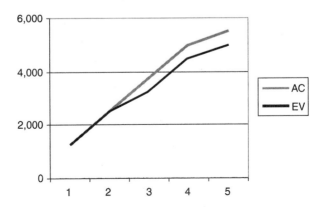

Figure 12.8 Cost Variance

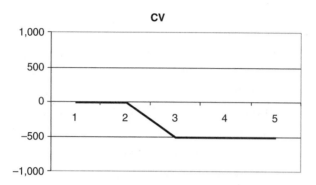

Figure 12.9 Cost Performance Index

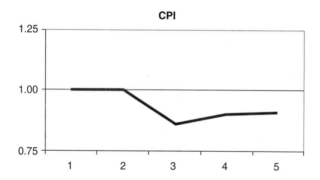

Figure 12.8 shows the cost variance, which is zero for the first two days but turns negative on day 3. The cost variance stays negative for the reminder of the project, indicating the cost overrun. Figure 12.9 shows the cost performance index, which signifies the same cost overrun.

Figure 12.10 shows the schedule variance, which turns negative on day 3, indicating the project is behind schedule. On day 5, the schedule variance returns to zero, because all of the work has been completed—the planned value is finally equal to the earned value. Figure 12.11 shows the schedule performance index, which shows the same behavior.

Figure 12.10 Schedule Variance

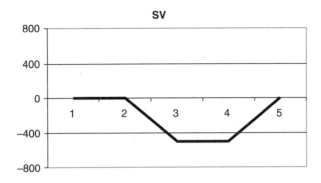

Figure 12.11 Schedule Performance Index

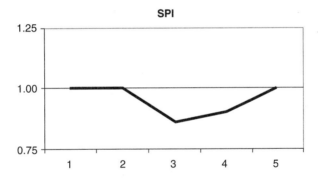

The SPI returns to 1.0 on day 5 as all of the work in the project is completed.

ESTIMATE TO COMPLETE

An important aspect of the earned value calculation is that it allows us to calculate a reasonable estimate for the cost to complete the project. Forecasting the final cost is difficult and depends on several assumptions. The most important issue to be resolved is whether the work required on the already completed activities is a reasonable predictor of the work required for the remaining activities.

Typical Variances

If the completed activities are running an average of ten percent over their planned value, is it reasonable to assume that the remaining activities will also require ten percent more than their planned value? If so, the variances for the completed activities are assumed to be typical, and an estimate of the project's final cost can be computed as follows:

$$ETC = \frac{(BAC - EV)}{CPI}$$

One first computes the value of the remaining activities. The remaining planned value can be found from the budget at completion (BAC) minus the earned value (EV). If we subtract the earned value of the work to date from the estimated total work, we get the value of the work remaining (BAC – EV). The estimate to complete (ETC) is found by dividing the remaining work by the CPI. A CPI of 0.9 says that the average cost of the activities to date is ten percent higher than planned. By dividing the estimate of the future work by 0.9 (or multiplying by 1.1), we increase the cost of the remaining work (BAC – EV), by ten percent.

That is, we assumed that the future work will follow the same pattern as the previous work, so we adjust the cost estimate of the future work to allow for the same change. The change is represented by the CPI. We determine the CPI for the previous work and apply it to the future work to get a more reliable estimate of the cost to complete the project. If we believe that performance on the past work is a reliable predictor of the future work, then we can use the CPI to predict the performance into the future.

Atypical Variances

If the completed activities are seen as atypical, then the project manager can assume that the estimate to complete (ETC) is simply the remaining planned value:

$$ETC = BAC - EV$$

In this case, the estimate to complete is the budget at completion minus the earned value to date. The trap here, of course, is that the project manager is assuming that the future performance will somehow change. For example, the CPI for the completed activities is 0.85, but the project manager assumes that it will magically improve to 1.25 for the rest of the project. Experience suggests that this is an unwise course. For most projects, past performance is an excellent predictor of future performance.

EARNED VALUE IN ACTION

Suppose your boss comes up to you and asks for an estimate of the progress of your project to date. What should you say?

Answer #1

We've had a few late assignments, but don't worry, we're going to make them up and everything will be back on schedule. We're also running under our scheduled costs, so we are in good shape.

Answer #2

As of last week, our budgeted cost was $300 for three deliverables. We've completed two, so our earned value is $200. It looks like the late assignment will get completed next week, so we are behind schedule. Out actual costs are $280, so we are also overrunning our costs.

Most project managers seem to give answer #1. Most politicians want to hear answer #1. From the completion of deliverables you understand the true status of the project. This is what you should report. The ethical standard signed by project management professionals (PMP) requires them to give answer #2.

TEST YOURSELF

Consider the following table of activities:

Activity	Predecessor	Duration (days)
Start	None	None
A	Start	4
B	Start	9
C	A	6
D	A, B	8
E	C, D	4
F	B, D	2
G	E, F	5
End	G	None

After nine days of work, activity A has been completed on time. Activity B has three deliverables and two have been completed. Assuming each day's work costs $100, what is the cost variance, the schedule variance, the CPI, and the SPI?

KEY POINTS TO REMEMBER

- The true status of a project is measured by completion of deliverables.
- The planned value, PV, is the baseline—it is the value of the work scheduled.
- The actual cost, AC, is the cost of work performed.
- The earned value, EV, is the value of the completed deliverables.
- Cost variance, $CV = EV - AC$.
- Schedule variance, $SV = EV - PV$.
- The cost performance index, $CPI = EV / AC$.
- The schedule performance index, $SPI = EV / PV$.
- $CPI > 1$ means the project is overrunning on cost.
- $SPI > 1$ means the project is behind schedule.

The Professional Project Manager

INTRODUCTION

The professional project manager today needs to have a level of comfort with the project management body of knowledge. The project manager should also be certified from a reputable program. In this chapter, we talk about both of these topics.

WHAT'S AHEAD

- The PMP credential
  - How to become certified
  - Application process
  - Sample exam questions
- Understanding the core topics
- Other global standards

IN THE REAL WORLD

In the mid 1990s, IBM formed its Project Management Center of Excellence (PMCOE) with the goal of introducing project management throughout the enterprise. IBM was a leader in the information technology (IT) field but they saw change coming. They noted that value was shifting in the IT industry, driven by the rising tide of global integration, a new computing paradigm, and new client needs.

IBM had to integrate their processes and standards with other global business and with different organizations around the world. They adopted a two-step process for the professional project manager at IBM. First, project professionals had to pass an external exam and earn a credential like the project management professional (PMP®), and then apply for the IBM PM certification. The former provided a strong foundation and international recognition for their employees. The internal examination within IBM broadly involved the candidate preparing a dossier with proof of project management experience. After personal interviews with the PMCOE certification board, candidates whose experience, skills, knowledge, and education were considered valid earned either certified senior project manager (CSPM) or certified executive project manager (CEPM).

This blended approach to certifying project managers is attractive, as you have the best of both worlds—an internationally recognized credential and verification of qualifications for being a productive project management professional within IBM itself.

KEY CONCEPTS

PMI administers several credentials, but the most popular and valuable is the project management professional (PMP). The PMP is a valuable credential that distinguishes employees not just within their own organizations but among the global project management and global business communities. The credentials that PMI manages are the following:

Program Management Professional (PgMP^SM)

This certification is for program managers—senior project managers responsible for the coordinated management of multiple related projects. Program managers possess the knowledge and skills needed to be effective in both the project and business or government environment and to make decisions that accomplish strategic objectives. They have advanced skills in finance, cross-cultural awareness, leadership, communication, influence, negotiation, and conflict resolution.

Project Management Professional (PMP®)

The PMP is a very valuable credential, assuring employers that the holder is committed to project management. Earning and maintaining this credential demonstrates a solid foundation in all aspects of project management. The PMP certifies that you have sufficient knowledge and experience to appropriately apply the right methodology to projects.

Certified Associate in Project Management (CAPM®)

The CAPM credential can benefit a wide range of individuals who want to demonstrate a comprehensive and consistent understanding of the application project management methods and enhance their contributions to the team's success.

Once you obtain your PMP or PgMP, you must maintain the credential through the Continuing Certification Requirements program. The credential is maintained through a series of activities, such as formal academic education courses, self-directed learning, attending courses offered by registered providers, and volunteering to professional or community organizations. PMP and PgMP professionals must acquire 60 professional development units (PDUs) in the three-year renewal cycle.

Finally, as professionals, you must adhere to the PMP Code of Ethics and Professional Conduct. Project managers must not only be competent, but must be committed to doing what is right and honorable. Project management professionals believe that embracing the code of ethics advances us both individually and professionally.

OBTAINING THE PMP

For students considering the PMP credential, we recommend the following approach. First, to be eligible to earn the PMP, you must have the following:

1. Either an associate's degree and five years of project management experience (during which, 7,500 hours were spent leading and directing project tasks) or a bachelor's degree and three years of project management experience (during which 4,500 hours were spent leading and directing project tasks).

2. Thirty-five contact hours of instruction in project management.

Once you have completed the forms to prove you have the required experience, you can apply to take the PMP exam, which consists of 200 multiple-choice questions to be answered in four hours. Of these, 25 are test questions used to evaluate future questions and are not counted in your score. There is a 15-minute tutorial before the test, which explains how everything works. PMI administers the test through computer-based testing (CBT). CBT centers are available in locations throughout the world. The entire process of application, payment, and scheduling of the test is easily accomplished online through the PMI website.

The Examination

The examination is comprised of 200 multiple-choice questions, and the allotted time to complete the examination is about four hours.

Test Breakdown by Areas

Domains	% of Items/Domain
I. Initiating the Project	11
II. Planning the Project	23
III. Executing the Project	27
IV. Monitoring and Controlling the Project	21
V. Closing the Project	9
VI. Professional Responsibility	9

Twenty-five questions inside the exam are not considered in the final score, as they are test questions only. You will not know which they are. They are randomly hidden in the test bank.

For more information, go to *www.pmi.org*. Here you will find further information concerning the project management professional certification (PMP) and certified associate in project management (CAPM).

Studying for the PMP Exam

Questions on the test break down into three categories: definitional, computational, and tricky. We have found that for our students (and ourselves!) the best approach is the following:

1. **Master the material in the PMBOK.**

   This looks easier than it actually is. The PMBOK is relatively easy to read and understand. However, it takes a while to understand that each and every paragraph can be the subject for a question. Consider the following paragraph taken directly from the PMBOK introduction:

   > High quality projects deliver the required product, service, or result within scope, on time, and within budget. The relationship among these factors is such that if any one of these three factors changes, at least one other factor is likely to be affected. Project managers also manage projects in response to uncertainty. Project risk is an uncertain event or condition that, if it occurs, has a positive or negative effect on at least one project objective.

   There are two definitions in the above paragraph: the one about the three factors, and the definition of risk. In between those definitions is a simple, easy-to-overlook sentence: "Project managers also manage projects in response to uncertainty." So while you are carefully concentrating on the two definitions, which are indeed important, the following question will catch you out:

   Project managers manage projects in response to:

   a. cost

   b. schedule

   c. performance

   d. uncertainty

   Answer: d. uncertainty

While the first three answers are actually correct, PMI insists that they are asking for the *best* answer. Appealing to the legal definition in the PMBOK, answer *d* is correct. In order to answer these types of questions correctly, we recommend the books in step 3 below.

2. **Take a course with a qualified institute.**

    A two-day course will be sufficient to cover all of the material in the test. This will provide you with the background to answer the definitional and computational types of questions. It will also prepare you to answer the tricky questions.

3. **Study the following resources.**

    The PMP exam contains many questions that are tricky unless you understand where they come from and what they are designed to achieve. To pass the exam, you need to be able to deal with these tricky questions. We recommend the following books, which you can study after completing your two-day course:

    a. *PMP® Exam Practice Questions and Solutions*, by Aileen Ellis, PMP. © AME Group, 2005. This book contains a series of questions that are well organized into sections corresponding to the PMBOK processes. This book will ensure that you clearly understand the basics. When you can answer these questions, you are ready to deal with the tricky ones.

    b. *PMP® Exam Prep*, by Rita Mulcahy, PMP. © RMC Publications, Inc., 2005. Rita's book takes a lot of time to master. Her approach is based on memorizing a large process chart, which allows you to figure out the inputs and outputs to the 44 processes. It's easier to memorize the chart than the names of the hundreds of documents that go into and out of the 44 processes.

WHY BECOME CERTIFIED?

The common responses we hear from various project managers to this question are recognition, challenge, requirement, and financial reward (cash bonus for becoming a PMP). Interviews with certified project managers also reveal that it has helped them master a common project management vocabulary.

Who can benefit from being a PMP? Virtually everyone involved in the project and program management field: project managers and other project team members, managers of project managers, customers and other project stakeholders, functional managers, educators teaching project management and related subjects, consultants and other specialists in project management and related fields, and program managers. Today program managers have their own credential from PMI if they wish to pursue it, called PgMP. Organizations like AT&T send their senior level employees to take the exam. They have several vice presidents who are PMPs.

EXPERIENCE VERIFICATION

To document your qualifications, you will be asked to complete an experience verification form as part of your PMI application. For the training component, you will document your skills by providing the institution name, the name of the course attended, the dates of attendance, and the contact hours earned. Any accredited university course in project management meets the experience criteria.

DOMAIN TOPICS IN THE EXAM

This section describes the domains that you will be tested on in the examination. They are in the specification documentation for the exam. The following are the domains that you will have to master:

- Initiating the Project
- Planning the Project
- Executing the Project
- Monitoring and Controlling the Project
- Closing the Project
- Professional and Social Responsibility

Initiating the Project

The key topics dealing with project initiation that you are responsible for in the exam include the following:

- Conduct project selection methods (e.g., cost benefit analysis, selection criteria) through meetings with the customer and experts, in order to evaluate the feasibility of new products or services.
- Define the scope of the project based on the business need, in order to meet the customer's project expectations.
- Document high-level risks, assumptions, and constraints using historical data and expert judgment, in order to understand project limitations.
- Perform key stakeholder analysis using brainstorming, organizational charts, interviewing techniques, and any available information, in order to gain buy-in and requirements for the success of the project.
- Develop the project charter through review with key stakeholders, in order to confirm project scope, risks, issues, assumptions, and constraints.

Planning the Project

For the planning domain you are responsible for mastering the following key concepts:

- Record detailed customer requirements, constraints, and assumptions with stakeholders, in order to establish the project deliverables using requirement-gathering techniques (e.g., planning sessions, brainstorming, focus groups) and the project charter.
- Create the work breakdown structure with the team using appropriate tools and techniques, in order to develop the cost, schedule, resource, quality, and procurement plans.
- Develop the change management plan by defining how changes will be handled, in order to manage risk.
- Obtain project plan approval from the customer, in order to formalize the project management approach.
- Conduct a kickoff meeting with all key stakeholders, in order to announce the start of the project, and review the overall project plan and gain consensus.

Executing the Project

The core concepts that you must master under project execution are the following:

- Execute the tasks as defined in the project plan, in order to achieve the project goals.
- Ensure a common understanding by setting expectations in accordance with the project plan, in order to align the stakeholders and team members.
- Implement the procurement of project resources in accordance with the procurement plan.
- Manage resource allocation proactively by ensuring that appropriate resources and tools are assigned to the tasks according to the project plan, in order to execute the planned tasks successfully.
- Implement the quality management plan to ensure that work is being performed according to required quality standards.
- Implement approved changes according to the change management plan, in order to ensure the successful completion and integration of all tasks.
- Implement the approved actions and work-arounds required to mitigate project risk events, in order to minimize the impact of the risks on the project.
- Improve team performance by building team cohesiveness, leading, mentoring, training, and motivating, in order to facilitate cooperation, ensure project efficiency, and boost morale.

Monitoring and Controlling the Project

The core concepts that you must master for monitoring and controlling projects are the following:

- Measure project performance using appropriate tools and techniques, in order to monitor the progress of the project, identify and quantify any variances, perform any required corrective actions, and communicate to all stakeholders.

- Ensure that project deliverables conform to quality standards established in the project quality plan using appropriate tools and techniques (e.g., testing, inspection, control charts), in order to adhere to customer requirements.

- Monitor the status of all identified risks by identifying any new risks, taking corrective actions, and updating the risk response plan, in order to minimize the impact of the risks on the project.

Closing the Project

The key closing concepts that you must master are the following:

- Formalize final acceptance for the project from the sponsor/customer by ensuring that the delivered product(s) and services comply with the agreed deliverables list, agreed scope, and any organizational procedures, in order to close contractual obligations and document the project's success.

- Obtain financial, legal, and administrative closure (e.g., final payments, warranties, contract sign-off) for internal and external vendors and customers using generally accepted accounting practices and SOX compliance, in order to ensure no further expenditure and to communicate formal project closure.

- Release all project resources using appropriate organizational policies and procedures (e.g., financial and human resources) and provide performance feedback, in order to make them available for other future project assignments.

- Communicate lessons learned by means of "post mortem" team discussions, 360-degree surveys, supplier performance evaluations, and workshops, in order to create and/or maintain knowledge and experience that could be used in future projects to improve overall project management processes, methodology, and decision-making, and to capitalize on best practices.

- Distribute the final project report using all project closure-related information, in order to highlight project variances, any open issues, lessons learned, and project deliverables, and to provide the final project status to all stakeholders.

- Archive project records, historical information, and documents (e.g., project schedule, project plan, lessons learned, surveys, risk and issues logs, etc.), in order to retain organizational knowledge, comply with statutory requirements, and ensure availability of data for potential use in future projects and internal/external audits.

- Measure customer satisfaction at the end of the project by capturing customer feedback using appropriate interview techniques and surveys, in order to gain, maintain, and improve customer long-term relationships.

Professional and Social Responsibility

The professional and social responsibility domain was introduced starting in 2000. The previous exams did not have questions on this domain. The key concepts you must master here are the following:

- Ensure personal integrity and professionalism by adhering to legal requirements, ethical standards, and social norms, in order to protect the community and all stakeholders and to create a healthy working environment.

- Enhance personal professional competence by increasing and applying knowledge, in order to improve project management services.

- Promote interaction among team members and other stakeholders in a professional and cooperative manner by respecting personal and cultural differences, in order to ensure a collaborative project management environment.

OTHER GLOBAL STANDARDS AND CERTIFICATIONS

In our "In the Real World" section of this chapter, we discussed IBM's approach to standards and certifications. Here we briefly introduce other organizations' standards and certification.

International Project Management Association (IPMA)

IPMA is an international federated body, predominantly based in Europe. It has several member organizations in Europe. Due to the diversity of business laws and regulations, each member is responsible for establishing its own national standards in the context of the baseline standards defined by the IPMA (the IPMA Competency Baseline, or ICB), as well as its own certification program, which is verified by the IPMA. The national societies serve the specific project management development needs of each country in its national language, while IPMA represents them as an umbrella organization at the international level for administrative purposes.

Let us review this for the United Kingdom's approach to certification and standards. The Association for Project Management (APM) is aligned with the International Project Management Association (IPMA) four-level certification program. The following qualifications, apart from the certificated project manager qualification, are delivered through APM-accredited training providers:

- Introductory certificate: For anyone looking to understand the principles of project management
- APMP (IPMA Level D): For people with up to two years of project management experience
- Practitioner qualification (IPMA Level C): For anyone with more than three years of project management experience
- Certificated project manager (IPMA Level B): For project managers with extensive experience in managing complex, multidisciplinary projects
- APM project risk management certificates: APM offers level-one and level-two certificates for project and program managers involved in project risk assessment in any way

Similarly, there are IPMA-accredited organizations in China and India. In some cases they have their own names. For example, in India, Project Management Associates is the registered professional body for project management, but has links with IPMA.

Australian Institute of Project Management (AIPM)

The AIPM is the national project management organization within Australia. They have adopted the PMBOK as the basis of their certification program. They have multiple levels of certification that are tied directly to the Australian government's Australian Qualifications Framework, a national program of qualification. AIPM offers the following certifications:

- Project team member/project specialist
- Project manager
- Project director/program manager

Association for the Advancement of Cost Engineering (AACE)

AACE was founded in 1956 in the United States and awards the CCE credential. It enables individuals to acquire professional capabilities within cost engineering. CCE is currently awarded only to those who hold a four-year degree from an accredited engineering program. The levels are:

- CCE: At least eight full years in the profession, of which up to four years may be substituted by an engineering degree or a PE license
- CCC: At least eight years of referral experience in the profession, of which up to four years may be substituted by a four-year degree in a related discipline
- ICC: At least four full years of experience in a cost/schedule-related field, of which up to four years may be substituted by appropriate college-level academic training

PRINCE2

PRINCE2™ is the United Kingdom de facto standard for project management, developed by the government and used in both the public and private sectors. The acronym stands for Projects IN Controlled Environments. PRINCE2 is now used by numerous private sector organizations both in the UK and worldwide and is mandatory on many European public sector projects.

The methodology was originally developed for use on IT projects, but since its relaunch as PRINCE2, it is used in any type of project. The ownership of PRINCE2 belongs to the Office of Government Commerce (OCG), and it is managed by the Association of Project Managers Group. PRINCE2 has a standard handbook with processes similar to the PM-BOK. A unique difference from the PMBOK is that PRINCE2 focuses on products and not the activities to produce them. This affects its method of planning, control, and execution. Regardless, there are three parts to the structure of each PRINCE2 method—processes, components, and techniques.

The Foundation is the first of the two PRINCE2 examinations you are required to pass to become a PRINCE2 practitioner. You have to demonstrate understanding of the principles and terminology of the method. Specifically, candidates must be able to describe the purpose and major content of all roles, the eight components, the eight processes and the sub-processes, and the techniques.

The Practitioner is the second of the two PRINCE2 examinations you are required to pass to become a PRINCE2 practitioner. The goal here is to measure whether a candidate would be able to apply PRINCE2 to the running and managing of a project within an organization.

TEST YOURSELF

It may be a valuable exercise at this stage to benchmark yourself against some of the questions that might appear in a project management certification exam. Check the answers after you have worked out all the examples.

Time Management

1. Slack is the amount of time that an activity may be delayed without affecting the:
   a. Early start of the succeeding activities
   b. Late start of the succeeding activities
   c. Project finish
   d. Cost of the project
   e. Late finish of any parallel activities

2. The most frequently used construct in the precedence diagramming method is:
   a. Start to start
   b. Finish to finish
   c. Start to finish
   d. Finish to start
   e. Dummy activity

Scope Management

3. Scope management is:
   a. Project control function
   b. Employed in change control
   c. A works authorization process
   d. Considered in cost, quality, and schedule
   e. All of the above

4. The scope document is generated during which stage?
   a. Initiating
   b. Planning
   c. Executing
   d. Controlling and monitoring
   e. Closing

Cost Management

5. Parametric estimates are based on variables such as:
   a. Detailed planning and cost restraints
   b. Physical characteristics and historical data
   c. The WBS and similar projects
   d. Project objectives and manpower allocations
   e. Precise measurements and multiple inputs

6. When comparing the cost of competing projects, which of the following is typically NOT considered?
   a. Opportunity costs
   b. Direct costs
   c. Sunk costs
   d. Indirect costs
   e. Burden rates

Risk Management

7. The purpose of project risk management is to:
   a. Identify those factors that will adversely impact project objectives
   b. Assess the impact of adverse project factors
   c. Assess the probability of adverse project factors
   d. a AND c
   e. All of the above

8. The Big Seven tools for quality management are found in the following process:
   a. Quality planning
   b. Quality assurance
   c. Quality control
   d. ISO 9000
   e. Guide to nonconformance documentation

Quality

9. Of the following, who has the ultimate responsibility for meeting project quality objectives?
   a. Project engineer
   b. Project manager
   c. Functional manager
   d. Quality assurance manager
   e. Project owner

10. What is the relative priority of project cost, schedule, and quality?
    a. 1) Cost - 2) Schedule - 3) Quality
    b. 1) Quality - 2) Schedule - 3) Cost
    c. 1) Quality - 2) Cost - 3) Schedule
    d. 1) Schedule - 2) Quality - 3) Cost
    e. All are of equal priority

Procurement

11. Fixed price contracts place more risk on the:
    a. Owner
    b. Buyer
    c. Seller
    d. Contractor
    e. c AND d

12. Which type of contract requires that the buyer keep the tightest labor/material cost control?
    a. Cost plus incentive fee
    b. Cost plus percentage of costs
    c. Cost plus fixed fee
    d. Firm fixed price
    e. Firm fixed price plus incentive

Human Resources

13. From the project manager's perspective, the best organizational structure to do a project is:
    a. Functional
    b. Strong matrix
    c. Weak matrix
    d. Balanced matrix
    e. Coordinator

14. The project manager spends the following range of time on project communications:
    a. 20–30%
    b. 30–50%
    c. 50–70%
    d. 70–90%
    e. Less than 20%

Communications Management

15. Communications is best described as:
    a. An exchange of information
    b. Providing written or oral directions
    c. Consists of senders and receivers
    d. Effective listening
    e. All of the above

The answers for the above questions are in the appendix. If you did not get more than 12 correct, do not be disappointed. The exam requires a lot of practice. With some guided preparation using a relevant study guide, you will be in good shape.

Acknowledgments

The material for this book grew out of courses we have taught at Boston University's Metropolitan College. We owe a debt of gratitude to Jay Halfond, Dean of MET College, and Tanya Zlateva, Associate Dean for Academic Programs, both for their foresight in supporting the growth of project management and for allowing us the room to innovate.

We also wish to thank Kip Becker, chair of the Department of Administrative Sciences, who has consistently pushed us to advance the academic quality of the project management program.

We wish to thank our colleagues in the Admin Sciences department for enduring endless staff meetings with PM agenda items: Bill Chambers, Jim Cormier, Sam Mendlinger, and John Sullivan, and to the newcomers, Ginny Greiman and Alon Raviv. We'd like to thank one of the best department staffs we've ever worked with, who make it possible for us to function on a daily basis: Lucille Dicker, Fiona Niven, Marlene Suarez, and Susan Sunde. In the Computer Science department, we would like to thank the Chairman Lou Chitkushev, Anatoly Temkin and Matt Slowik. The two full-time colleagues actively involved in the project management program Eric Braude, and Bob Schudy and other members of the department have been very supportive. Two colleagues, Leo Burstein and Rosemary Antonucci, who helped with introducing a blended version of IT Project Management course, need to be acknowledged as well.

The staff at MET College's Distance Education department have been considerate and supportive colleagues. Thanks to Susan Krzyczka, Steve Hufsmith, Brad Kay Goodman, Rachel Wilder, and Nancy Coleman (even though she's moved on). The various staff who helped with managing our online classes and the facilitators who helped to teach our project management curriculum deserve our appreciation. Within this context, the students and practitioners, who have come across our paths either face-to-face or virtually, deserve our appreciation.

We'd like to thank the entire Kaplan team for getting us through the daunting process of delivering the book: Shannon Berning, Acquisitions Editor for guiding us through the contract, and Josh Martino, Associate Acquisitions Editor, for his thorough and persistent editing, conducted with gentle grace. Fred Urfer as production editor was wonderful to work with and shaped the final version of this book. We would like to thank the reviewers who provided valuable comments in shaping the book—Eugene Kaluzniacky, and Shawn O'Donnell.

Finally, we want to acknowledge the support of our family members, and the encouragement of our long-suffering wives, Dina Kanabar and Eileen Warburton, who put up with us as we yet again burnt the midnight oil.

Appendix A: Test Yourself Answers

CHAPTER 1: INTRODUCTION TO PROJECT MANAGEMENT

Answer for 1.1

a.   While cooking a unique vegan meal for the first time can be a project, cooking the regular lunch or dinner in a restaurant is not a project.

b.   Building a boat is a project. Operating a marina is an operation and not a project.

c.   Upgrading your OS is a project unless you are working in IT and do this for a living. Playing a video game is not a project.

Answer for 1.2

1.   A 50th wedding anniversary is a project and getting married is a project.

2.   Creating a new product is a project.

3.   Studying for the Project Management Exam is a project.

4.   Working in payroll and sending out a check for the first time to a new vendor is not a project.

5.   Writing a book is a project (no kidding!), but sending out weekly newsletters is not a project.

6.   Creating a new online course on HIPAA compliance at your company and presenting it for the first time could be a project; teaching the same course again is not a project.

Answer for 1.3

- Investing in planning which results in projects completing on time and under budget
- Establishing success criteria ahead of time gives specific criteria for measuring costs and schedules

- Aligning projects with strategy results in useful and valuable projects
- Saves money by preventing rework—due to sound project quality management
- Focusing on communications management results in happier stakeholders
- Faster time-to-market due to timely completion of deliverables
- Proper planning which ensures that there is compliance with standards and regulations
- Fewer surprises and issues due to risk management
- Due to communication processes all parties are aware of what is happening
- Ability to react to changes effectively

Answer for 1.4

You may have answers such as the following:

- A good communicator
- A leader (proactive style)
- Able to work well under pressure
- Goal-oriented
- Knowledgeable about the company
- Experienced (coaching, swift decision makes, resource manager)
- A manager and administrator
- An innovator
- Technically competent, respected, and aware

CHAPTER 2: PROJECT MANAGEMENT: A CASE STUDY

Answer for 2.1

A project manager will likely be spending the most amount of his time in the planning phase, followed by the monitoring and control phase. The latter will be larger for large projects.

CHAPTER 3: PROJECT INITIATION: THE SCOPE

Answer for 3.1

Introduction

There are several parts to a complete scope. First, there is the description of the requirements—what the party is intended to achieve. Then there are all the elements of the scope that are in the checklist:

- Project description
- The justification or opportunity
- Goals and objectives
- Deliverables
- Milestones
- Assumptions
- Limits and constraints
- The statement of work
- The customer interface

Not all sections are applicable to all projects. However, if a section is not applicable, it should still be listed in the document, with the added comment that the section does not apply.

50th Anniversary Party Project
Scope Document

Project Description

(We begin with the general requirements that set the tone.)

The project is to plan and hold a party for my friends' 50th anniversary party. They are so busy that they have asked me to help. The 50th anniversary is a special event, but the first thing to realize is that the couple is probably in their seventies, and this affects the type of party.

The guests include children and grandchildren, who will be coming from far away, and so a weekend date is more convenient. A wide range of ages will be present, so a variety of activities and arrangements is appropriate.

The most flexible combination for the party, therefore, is an afternoon garden party in a nice hotel. This allows for multiple rooms and an outside garden area. A sit-down meal is too formal and will prevent people from mingling, so a buffet is proposed. This will also reduce the cost and at the same time, allow for a more varied and flexible menu.

Other requirements are the following: A photographer to record the event; Music is not needed; and Taxi service home for the anniversary couple.

The Justification or Opportunity
(Typically this would be the company's opportunity to make money on the project. This section is not particularly relevant to this project.)

This is a once-in-a-lifetime opportunity to celebrate a rare event, so every effort will be made to make the day special.

Goals and Objectives
The objective is to have a classy, special event and for all the close family and selected friends to attend. The number of people is estimated to be 45.

The photographer will take pictures of each family with the anniversary couple. Guests will be allowed to consume alcohol in the hotel bar. Champagne will be served with the cutting of the cake.

Deliverables
- Party plan including schedule
- Invitations
- Reservation list
- Contract with the hotel
- Contract with the photographer
- Menu for the buffet
- Anniversary cake
- Photographs

Milestones
(Milestones are often in terms of actual dates, but it is easier in the planning stage to use days after the beginning of the project, particularly if the actual date is not known.) e.g.,

- Project plan, 14 days
- Invitations, day 30
- Hotel contract, day 45
- Photographer contract, day 45

- Buffet menu, day 60
- Order flowers for anniversary couple, day 80
- Pay photographer, day 90
- Receive photographs, day 100

Assumptions, Limits, and Constraints

(This section is often overlooked, but it is a useful place to detail what is not to be covered. Thinking about these issues often helps clarify the responsibilities and minor details.)

- Transportation to the event is the responsibility of the guests. (At this point, we might ask how the anniversary couple is to get to the event, and perhaps a limousine is appropriate. This is an example of the type of refinement of the scope that happens during detailed planning.)
- Camera and lighting equipment is the responsibility of the photographer.
- Local alcohol laws and restrictions are the responsibility of the hotel.

The Statement of Work

(The SOW usually applies to projects with detailed contracts between the buyer and the seller. In this case, an SOW is overkill.)

There is no SOW for this project.

The Customer Interface

Two people are primarily involved in the planning of the event: Roger and Gillian, both children of the couple. It has been decided that Gillian will arrange the hotel, the guests, and the food. Roger will organize the entertainment, including speeches and photographs. He will assign the speeches and plan the gift. Roger and Gillian will talk once a week to make sure that they cover everything.

Conclusions

Did you include all of these details? If you did, your party is likely to go much smoother. If not, people are likely to be running around at the last minute. Also, it is very useful to send the scope document to several people. In this case, all of the children may well feel that they have a stake in this party and have important things to contribute. Such stakeholder management is a key part of project management. Finally, stakeholders will often catch the missing items, and the scope document will be much better for their input. Don't forget to assign someone to pick up the cake!

CHAPTER 4: PROJECT PLANNING PART I: THE WORK BREAKDOWN STRUCTURE

Answer for 4.1

50th Anniversary Party Project Work Breakdown Structure (WBS)

The key thing to remember is that the WBS is a deliverable-oriented breakdown. It includes all of the activities that make up the project. The majority of these activities come from the scope, but they can also come from other places. In particular, project management activities are part of the project, so they belong in the WBS. (Did you remember to include the PM activities in your WBS?)

The high-level breakdown is best presented in graphical format, as shown in figure A4.1. Note:

- All of the activities are described in terms of verbs.

- Not all levels of the WBS are completed to the same level. Only as much detail as is appropriate is provided at this stage.

- The "Organize Food" activity does not involve cooking or serving. That has been assigned to the hotel. If the hotel is not doing the cooking and serving, then either the

Figure A4.1 High-Level WBS for 50th Anniversary Party in Graphical Format

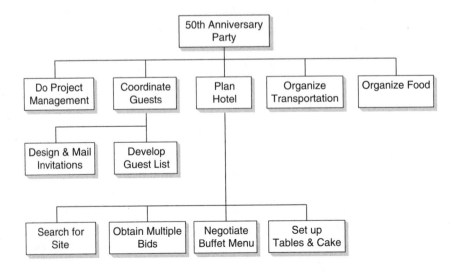

Figure A4.2 Lower-Level Detail for WBS in Graphical Format.

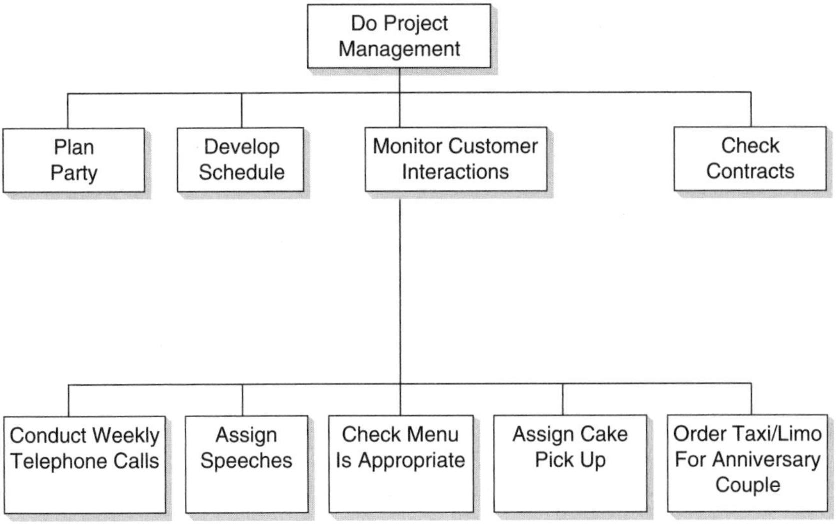

activity name must be changed (e.g., "Plan and Serve Food") or another activity must be added (e.g., "Serve Food").

More detail can be supplied in graphical format, for example in figure A4.2. Lower levels are best presented in the outline format, as shown in table A4.1.

Table A4.1: Lower-Level Detail for WBS in Outline Format

1.0	50th Anniversary Party
1.1	Do project management.
1.2	Coordinate guests.
1.3	Plan hotel.
1.4	Organize transportation.
1.5	Organize food.
	1.5.1 Select bids from hotel.
	1.5.2 Determine culinary restrictions (diabetics, vegetarians, etc.).
	1.5.3 Pick menu consistent with budget.
	1.5.4 Select number of tables.
	1.5.5 Check food upon arrival.

CHAPTER 5: PROJECT PLANNING PART II: THE NETWORK

Answer for 5.1

1. The network diagram is shown in Figure A5.1.

Figure 5.1 Network diagram

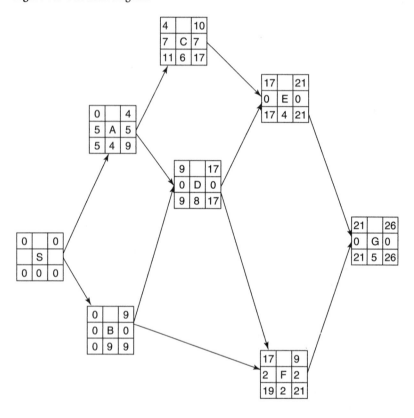

2. What activities are on the critical path?

    Start, B, D, E, G, End

3. If the customer wants to have the project finished in 24 days, what would you recommend?

    B and D are the longest tasks on the CP, so work to shorten them.
    This answer is not unique—you can have any sort of plan that takes two days out of the critical path schedule.

CHAPTER 6: PROJECT EXECUTION, AND MONITORING AND CONTROL

Answer for 6.1

Profit Calculation

a.   If the project finishes one month early, what is your fee percentage?

The project costs $100,000 for 12 months, so it costs $8,333 per month. If you finish a month early, then you spend 11 × $8,333 = $91,666.

The fee is $10,000, and you are entitled to that for finishing the project. However, the customer has also said that the reward for an early finish is $5,000 split equally between you. Therefore, you are entitled to another $2,500 for finishing a month early, and the total fee is $10,000 + $2,500 = $12,500.

The percentage fee is the fee divided by the costs:

$$\text{Percentage Fee} \quad = \quad \frac{12,500}{91,666} \quad = \quad 13.6\%$$

b.   If the project finishes one month late, what is your fee percentage?

If you finish a month late, then you probably spend an extra $8,333, for a total cost of $108,333. The late penalty is $10,000 and you must also pay this, so your total costs are $118,333.

The fee is $10,000, and you are entitled to that for finishing the project. The percentage fee is the fee divided by the total costs:

$$\text{Percentage Fee} \quad = \quad \frac{10,000}{118,333} \quad = \quad 8.5\%$$

Answer for 6.2

Critical Path Issue

The relevant part of the critical path is shown in Figure A6.1: The important feature of the critical path is that if any activity is delayed, then all of the following activities are delayed,

Figure A6.1 Critical Path Activities.

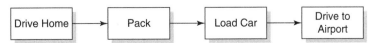

and the entire project is delayed. Therefore, if you get held up at work by an hour, the project will be delayed by an hour. You will arrive at the airport an hour after your plan. It is possible, therefore, that you will miss the flight—a really bad idea for an anniversary trip!

How can we reduce the risk? There are several possibilities:

1. Pack in the morning before you leave for work. This eliminates the "Pack" activity from the critical path and allows more time in case you are held up at work.

2. You can also load your luggage into the car. This may not complete the "Load Car" activity, as your spouse may take the day off and pack while you are at work. However, this will reduce the length of the activity somewhat.

3. If you are really late, then you can have your spouse meet you at the airport, and instead of driving home, you can take a taxi from work to the airport. You may well dressed in your work suit while everyone else is in shorts and T-shirts, but at least you will make the trip.

Notice that we concentrate on critical path activities *only* in our analysis. There is no point in worrying about any activities that are not on the critical path, such as eating lunch.

CHAPTER 7: CLOSING AND CONTRACTS

Answer for 7.1

Pharmaceutical contract: Pharmaceuticals take a long time to develop, and the risks are very high that the drug will not be successful. Also, testing on humans is an expensive, complicated process, and the regulations are very strict. Because the uncertainties are huge, the contract type that is appropriate is a cost plus contract.

It may be appropriate to include incentives. The subcontractor may have done this type of testing before and so may have access to documentation that is very similar and that can be reused. If the critical path is driven by the completion of documentation, then incentives for early completion may be appropriate.

Answer for 7.2

Building a two-car garage: If the house already exists, then this is a fairly straightforward project. The area is known, and there are likely to be several contractors who can do the job. Therefore, a fixed price contract is an option. The contractor may not agree to such a contract, but may agree to negotiate about add-ons and any surprises.

Answer for 7.3

Building a road: In the past, road contracts were almost always cost plus contracts. However, municipal governments have become much smarter in this area, and now often negotiate incentive fee contracts. Since road construction adds delays for commuters, the contractor will be rewarded for finishing early, and penalized for finishing late. However, the specification needs to be very good so that it is clear what kind of foundation exists, what road surface is required, whether bridges are involved, etc.

Answer for 7.4

Conducting a campaign for charity: Most charitable organizations have very little money. Therefore, they will almost always select a fixed price contract. Nonprofit organizations cannot deal with the potential for cost overruns associated with cost plus contracts.

Answer for 7.5

Closing the party involves closing all of the contracts. In this case, the contracts are with the hotel, the photographer, and the taxi drivers. Therefore, the closing activities are the following:

- Pay hotel bill.
- Pay photographer.
- Pay taxi driver.

CHAPTER 8: PROJECT COMMUNICATIONS

Answer for 8.1

There are several good choices. Expert power is a good choice for a project manager. Using referent power to motivate the team also works. If it is a projectized structure or strong matrix structure, legitimate power will also work for the project manager. Coercive power will usually not work.

Answer for 8.2

Team members must be good at communicating and influencing the project manager. They should communicate how the manager's management style is a deterrent to project progress.

Answer for 8.3

For a project manager, having good communication skills and people skills is very important. Typically, the team members are hired for their technical skills, and the project manager is hired for his/her management skills.

Answer for 8.4

Conflict Resolution Worksheet

Conflict Participants	Name: Joe	Name: Mary
Problem:	Joe feels that complete prototype must be built before development begins because the technology is untried and risky.	Mary says that there is no time to prototype, and building a prototype will impact the schedule.
Preferred Solution:	Assign two resources two weeks to complete the prototype. It is possible that the time can be saved later on by reusing parts of the prototype.	Mary feels that the problems can be solved by consulting outside sources and that the issues likely to arise have been solved before.

Options to Resolve This Conflict

	Option	Consequence
1.	Extend the deadline of the project after asking the sponsor if this is acceptable.	Delay in project completion. Mary will not have any issue with this solution if the sponsor accepts a delayed completion date.
2.	Replace part of the technology that is untried.	Not sure if this will introduce other risks. Not sure if the new technology will be a good fit.
3.	Get additional resources to help. Consider outsourcing. Divide work among team members to complete the prototype.	This should not impact the solution. There is no budget for outsourcing the project.
4.	Create a partial prototype. Test out the uncertain features.	This will not take too much time from the schedule. Also, it will allow us to determine if the technology is feasible. Mary has no objection to partial prototyping.

Conclusion: After brainstorming several solutions, Joe and Mary are happy with solution 4. Conflict resolved.

CHAPTER 9: PROJECT COST ESTIMATION

Answer for 9.1

The bottom-up estimate is likely to be more accurate. The reason for this is that for a bottom up estimate, the WBS has to be decomposed into small units. Smaller units are usually more clearly identified and can be more accurately estimated.

Answer for 9.2

Top-down estimation is faster than bottom-up estimation. Top-down estimation is performed during the early stages of the project when the sponsor needs to be given a good ballpark estimate. If there are well-defined and calibrated parametric models available, the level of accuracy for top- down estimates may be quite good.

Answer for 9.3

Parametric models use a predictor for estimation of effort or cost. In project domains where the predictor is well established based on history, the model is accurate. The model provides a quick way to generate an estimate that is reliable if adjusted for project complexity and project team experience. What are the weaknesses? We will not get accurate estimates if the model is not updated constantly or if it is being used for estimating a project that is a poor fit for the model.

Answer for 9.4

It is not possible to come up with an estimate that is close to 100 percent.

However, techniques such as the three-point method will give a mean, which when added with three standard deviations and adjusted for project complexity can result in a pretty reliable estimate.

CHAPTER 10: PROJECT RISK MANAGEMENT

Answer for 10.1

Most organizations will be using a slightly modified template from what was introduced in this chapter and is shown in the figures that follow. They all should have risk identification, risk quantification, risk response plans, and risk contingency plans.

Figure A10.1 Risk Identification and Quantification Template

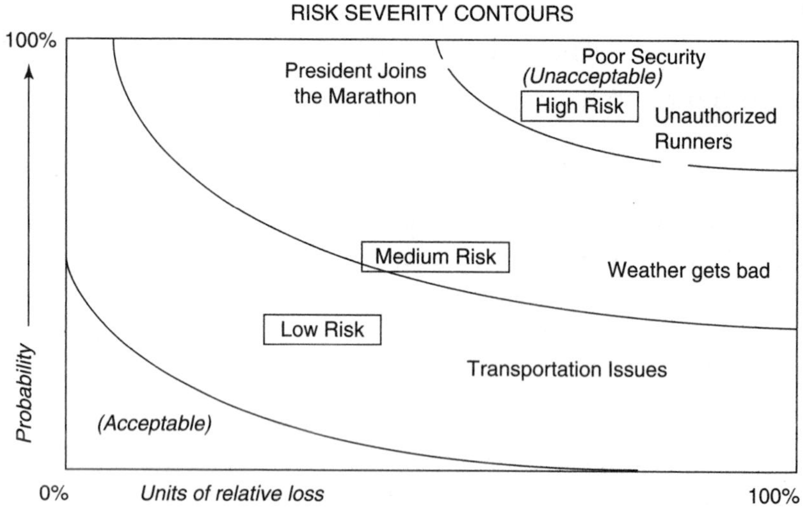

Answer for 10.2

For example: communication risk, scope creep, quality risk. Mitigation for communication risk could be having a comprehensive communication plan—the contingency plan should be to escalate issues with a supervisor or stakeholder. Mitigation for scope creep could be to have a formal change control plan and to stick with it. Quality risk can be mitigated by having a good quality management plan and a plan for quality control.

Answer for 10.3

Five risks could be the following: president decides to participate in the marathon; weather gets really bad; unauthorized runners; transportation issues; and event security.

Answer for 10.4

Risk Response

Risk	Risk Response
President Clinton Participates	• Identify contingency staff of 12 people. • Dedicate a person to establish lines of communication with presidential security staff.
Bad Weather	• Allocate a person to monitor for storms, as well as unusally warm or cold weather; and communicate to runners about conditions and/or possible delays via cell phone.

Transportation and/or Traffic Problems	• Research and publicize alternate ways to transport runners and spectators. • Develop transportation tips for walking, driving, airport transport, taxi, and public transport. Plan to make tips widely available and publicize via local press.
Event Security Breakdown	• Allocate contingency staff of 100 people to work in command and control center and on the course in the event of a security problem. • Install security devices and cameras at key points. • Get best security practice results from large events. • Develop relations with Department of Homeland Security, police, FBI, etc. • Develop response plans for several types of incidents. • Create and test communication channels to be used for security incidents. • Conduct simulation of a security crisis event.
Unauthorized Runners	• Assign unique RFID electronic devices for runners to wear at all times. • Check for authorized runners at key points. • Plan for handling bandits.

Answer for 10.5

Risk Contingency Plans

Risk	Response
President Participates	Activate contingency staff and contingency plan to work closely with president's security detail.
Bad Weather	Send emails and text messages to cell phones of all participants. Inform local media about the scheduled changes.
Transportation Issues	Delay start and inform all participants using communication channels identified above.
Event Security	Activate the appropriate security plan for the incident response. Activate communication channels for response to security incidents.
Unauthorized Runners	Security politely removes unauthorized runners. If there are further problems the police are involved.

CHAPTER 11: PROJECT QUALITY MANAGEMENT

Answer for 11.1

If there is an emphasis on quality in the company vision statement, that is a good sign. This should be backed up with resources for quality planning, quality assurance, and quality control from the organization leaders. Also, do you have quality documents that have to be completed in all projects? Are they visible? Are they mandatory? If so, you have a quality-first attitude in the organization.

Answer for 11.2

Quality is part of the triple constraint. If you don't manage the three constraints of scope, cost, and time concurrently, you risk sacrificing two of the three constraints. There is also a tight link between time and cost. If the time is extended, the budget gets blown. A good magic solution would be to reduce project scope. From our experience, while projects have scope creep, many have some scope that was designed in but is no longer relevant to the project. The project manager can save time, money, and cost (and preserve quality) by asking the following questions about functionality and features at various milestones: "What must be implemented next?" and "What would be nice to implement next?" The "nice to implement" feature should be removed for now, and this immediately translates into scope reduction, which in turn reduces constraints on cost and time. The team members can now focus on quality deliverables.

Answer for 11.3

Quality Item	Measurable Item	Unit of Measure
Reliability: Zero Defects and Stable Software	• Error reports • Downtime	• Mean time between failures • % downtime < 1%
Security	Unauthorized logins	Zero unauthorized logins
Robust Application and Forms	Number of defects	Zero defects is the goal. Greater than 5% will be acceptable.
Documentation	Number of defects in documentation	Zero defects is the goal. Greater than 5% will be acceptable.
User-Friendly Ability	Usability index: Users are asked to rate website usability	1= Excellent and 5 = Poor

Answer for 11.4

A quality plan for a software project would have details on the following items:
1. Introduction

    1.1. Project overview

    1.2. Project scope

    1.3. Testing

    1.4. Completion criteria

    1.5. Schedule

2. Test matrix

    2.1. QA methodologies

    2.2. Test summary report

3. Test plan

    3.1. Activities

    3.2. Resources

4. Traceability matrix

5. Test cases

6. Test scripts

7. Defect reports

8. Quality risk assessment

9. Performance and stability test plan

CHAPTER 12: ADVANCED PROJECT PLANNING

Answer for 12.1

This is the same table as in figure 5.1 in chapter 5. It may help to look at the network diagram there. Activity A has been completed in four days on time. So the cost of A is $400. Activity B should have taken nine days and should be complete, but B has actually cost $900, and we have only accomplished two-thirds of the deliverables.

Actual Cost: AC = $400 + $900 = $1,300

Planned Value: PV = $400 + $900 = $1,300

Now let's turn to the earned value:

A is complete, so the activity has "earned" $400.

B is two-thirds complete, so it has "earned" 2/3 × $900 = $600.

We emphasize that you only "earn" the value of the 100% completed deliverables. Because only two out of three deliverables have been completed, you have only earned two-thirds of the cost, or $600. (We are assuming that the deliverables are all of equal value.)

Earned Value: EV = $400 + $600 = $1,000

We can now use the formulas for the cost variance (CV), the schedule variance (SV), the cost performance index (CPI), and the schedule performance index (SPI):

$$CV = EV - AC = 1,000 - 1,300 = -300$$
$$CPI = EV/AC = 1,000/1,300 = 0.7692 = 0.77$$
$$SV = EV - PV = 1,000 - 1,300 = -300$$
$$SPI = EV/PV = 1,000/1,300 = 0.7692 = 0.77$$

The question states that each DAY has a value of $100 (not each activity). Therefore, activity A has a value of $400, not $100.

CHAPTER 13: THE PROFESSIONAL PROJECT MANAGER

Answer for 13.1

1. A
2. D
3. B
4. B
5. B
6. C
7. E
8. C
9. B
10. E
11. E
12. B
13. B
14. D
15. E

Appendix B: Resources

FURTHER READING

For students who wish to learn more about the methods of project management, we recommend the following textbook: *Project Management, the Managerial Process,* by Clifford Gray and Erik Larson (McGraw-Hill-Irwin, Fourth Ed., 2008). The book is easy to read, covers a broad variety of topics, and has many good problems for further study. The chapters on project networks, one of the more challenging topics, are particularly good.

The Project Management Institute (PMI®) website is a wonderful resource for information about all aspects of project management: *www.pmi.org.* The Resources section is full of information on research, publications, and standards. There is also extensive information on career development, certifications, and jobs. The James R. Snyder Center for Project Management Knowledge & Wisdom contains a catalog of PMI-published literature and books. It is an excellent place to start looking for the information you need.

REFERENCES

Chapter 1

Project Management Institute (2004), *A Guide to the Project Management Body of Knowledge* (PMBOK), Third Edition, Newtown Square, PA.

Webster's dictionary entry for the term *project* is at *www.webster.com.*

The Dunkin Donut's zero trans fat project is described in *The Boston Globe,* Sept 16, 2007, by Jenn Abelson, "The long, secret journey to a healthier donut." *www.boston.com/business/articles/2007/09/16/the_long_secret_journey_to_a_healthier_donut* and *www.dunkindonuts.com/aboutus/ press/PressRelease.aspx?viewtype=current&id=100102*

A review of project manager job descriptions was based on information at *www.mariosalexandrou.com/free-job-descriptions/project manager.asp.*

Chapter 2

Kathy Schwalbe (2007), *Information Technology Project Management*, Fifth Edition, course technology, MA.

Abhishek Trigunait helped with the initial preparation of the Project Vista case study. Veena Naga Prashanthi Kanumilli assisted with the MS Project implementation of the Vista case study.

Chapter 3

More details on the "Elements of the Scope" can be found in *Project Management, the Managerial Process*, by Clifford Gray and Erik Larson.

The data in figure 3.2 is taken from: *Software Engineering Economics* (1981), by Barry Boehm, Prentice Hall.

Kuffel, W., "Extra time saves money," *Computing Language*, December 1990.

Dean Leffingwell's Web page entitled "Calculating your return on investment from more effective requirements management" can be found at *www.ibm.com/developerworks/rational/library/347.html*.

Sheldon, F. et al, "Reliability Measurement from Theory to Practice," *IEEE Software*, July 1992.

Chapter 4

More details on the WBS can be found in *Project Management, the Managerial Process*, by Clifford Gray and Erik Larson.

Chapter 5

More details on the network diagram method can be found in *Project Management, the Managerial Process*, by Clifford Gray and Erik Larson. The notation in this chapter is that proposed by Gray and Larson and so should be easy for a reader of this chapter to understand.

Chapter 6

The statistics on the Big Dig are taken from the Massachusetts Turnpike Authority (MTA), website *www.masspike.com/bigdig*. This site is a treasure trove of information about the Central Artery Tunnel project.

A useful overview of the costs and risks for the Big Dig were provided to us by Virginia A. Greiman in an article entitled "The Central Artery/Tunnel Project Overview of Cost, Risks and Quality," March 11, 2008.

The data on the costs overruns on the Big Dig in figure 6.2 can be found in a Bechtel/ Parsons Brinckerhoff report from December 2006, entitled "The Big Dig: Key Facts About Cost, Scope, Schedule and Management" available at *www.bechtel.com/assets/files/PDF/ BostonTunnel/BigDig_KeyFacts_Dec2006.pdf.*

An interesting article on lessons learned is "Sharing Experiences and Lessons Learned," by Chris Allen and Phil E. Barnes, at the U.S. Department of Transportation, Federal Highway Administration, website *www.tfhrc.gov/pubrds/04jul/09.htm.*

Chapter 8

The opening case study on communications in the real world is from Jim Cormier.

The MLB in Japan case study is described in *The Boston Globe* article, "It was a time for team unity," by Jackie MacMullan, March 20, 2008.

Chapter 9

The opening case study on communications in the real world is from Virginia Greiman.

Additional references for this chapter are:

Kayser, Thomas (1994), *Team Power: How to Unleash the Collaborative Genius of Work Teams.* McGraw-Hill.

French, J.R.P. and Raven, B. (1959), "The bases of social power," in D. Cartwright (ed.), *Studies in Social Power.* Ann Arbor, MI: University of Michigan Press.

Chapter 10

The opening case study on Bill Gates is from Microsoft archives.

A useful summary of risk management with a software project focus can be found at: Alex Down, Michael Coleman, Peter Absolon (1994), *Risk Management for Software Projects*, McGraw-Hill-Irwin.

The closing case study based on the 100th Boston Marathon is taken from *The Hartford Courant* article by Lori Riley, staff writer (Monday, April 15, 1996).

Chapter 11

The opening case study is based on an *International Herald Tribune article*, August 8, 2006.

The closing case study is taken from a report on the Big Dig by Virginia Greiman.

Chapter 12

An excellent introductory book, which covers earned value in detail, is *Earned Value Project Management*, Third Edition, by Quentin W. Fleming and Joel M. Koppelman, published by the Project Management Institute, 2006.

Chapter 13

References on the opening case study can be found at Beyond the PMP.

Advanced project management certification by Kevin Aguanno is available at *www. pmforum.org/library/papers/2002/AdvancedPMCertAguanno.pdf.*

The exam specifications are from the Project Management Institute (2005), Project Management Professional (PMP*) Examination Specification, Newtown Square, PA.

The data on PMP certification processes and the sample test questions are from the PMI website, viewed on March 1, 2008.

Other certification information can be found at:

PRINCE2—Projects IN Controlled Environments. Retrieved March 30, 2008, from website *www.prince2.org.uk/home/home.asp.*

IPMA Member Associations. Retrieved March 30, 2008, website *www.asapm.org/ipma/ipma_ma.asp.*

AIPM. Retrieved March 30, 2008, website *www.aipm.com.au.*

Association for Project Management. Retrieved March 30, 2008, website *www.apm. org.uk.*

PMI. Retrieved March 30, 2008, website *www.pmi.org/Pages/default.aspx.*

Index

Page numbers in *italics* refer to tables and figures.

About the Authors

Vijay Kanabar

A certified Project Management Professional, Vijay Kanabar, BSc, MS, MBA, PMP, PhD, is Director, of Boston University's Metropolitan College's Project Management programs. He is an Associate Professor in the department of Administrative Sciences and Computer Science jointly, where he teaches Information Technology and Project Management courses. He has been recognized with awards for outstanding teaching and research and has consulted with several Fortune 500 corporations in the area of IT and project management consultant. He received his BSc in India from the University of Madras, his PhD in Canada from the University of Manitoba, and his MBA and MS in the United States from Webber and Florida Institute of Technology respectively.

Roger D. H. Warburton

Roger Warburton is an Associate Professor in the Department of Administrative Sciences at Boston University's Metropolitan College. He teaches undergraduate courses in project management and operations management, and graduate courses in project management and supply chain management. His project management research focuses on the theory and modeling of techniques for improving earned value management. In his supply chain research, he designs practical, useful methods for controlling inventory in response to the modern consumer's ever-changing needs and desires. He recently discovered the exact solutions to the supply chain equations and published a series of papers on the topic. Before changing careers becoming a professor at B.U., he worked in a series of consulting positions in Information Technology projects in the defense industry, and most recently, the apparel industry. He received an MS and PhD in Physics from the University of Pennsylvania, and a BSc in Physics from Sussex University in the U.K. He is a certified project management professional (PMP).

Your MBA Experience

If you are reading this book, you may be wondering if you should pursue an MBA degree and what the business school experience might be like.

Is the MBA right for you?

The decision to go to business school can be difficult, as it's a significant investment of time and money, and it can dramatically alter your career path. According to GMAC, the company that administers the GMAT exam for MBA applicants, the most commonly-cited reasons for pursuing an MBA are the opportunity for more challenging work, personal satisfaction, long-term financial stability, and the desire to remain marketable. Whatever your reasons for pursing business school, an MBA provides the opportunity to develop extensive leadership, teamwork, and management experience in 1-2 years.

How can an MBA benefit your career?

Over 80% of MBA graduates say that they could not have obtained their present job without their MBA, and even though the degree requires a steep up-front investment, most MBA graduates see a positive return on their investment within about five years of graduating.

Some grads use the MBA to completely change their careers, and others use it to accelerate their current career progression. While consulting and financial services account for about 50% of job offers at most schools, MBA degrees are increasingly useful for advancing careers in a wide variety of fields. In fact, many MBA programs actively recruit prospective students from less traditional fields, such as media, entertainment, healthcare, and public service. Any business or institution needs strong managers, and an MBA degree provides a well-rounded background in management and business skills that can be applied throughout your career.

What is business school really like?

Course work

Did you study business as an undergrad? Although topics in business school will sound familiar, the approach taken with each subject will be more strategic than when you studied subjects like finance, statistics, and marketing as an undergraduate.

You've never taken a business class? Not a problem—the MBA degree is designed for students from a wide variety of different backgrounds. While some of your potential classmates may be more familiar with terminology in specific disciplines, the material will be taught so that anyone has the potential to learn and apply it effectively. Furthermore, many b-schools will offer a pre-MBA course or set of courses for those who have not studied business before, which can be very helpful.

Learning through case studies and study groups

Studying during your MBA program would likely be different than your undergraduate coursework. Many courses use case studies as the primary tool for learning. A case study is a detailed description of a specific business issue at a specific company, or in a specific industry. Extensive background is often, but not always, included in a case study, and your goal is to review all of the information, extract the relevant data and issues, and come to class prepared to discuss the situation's challenges and the steps you would consider if you were in the management situation. A large portion of your learning would come from discussion with your peers and professors through hearing their perspectives and personal experiences with similar situations.

Business school involves spending a lot of time in study groups. What better preparation is there for the global business world than to work in a study group of 4-6 new colleagues of different ages, backgrounds, career paths, and often nationalities, and to complete projects together? Study groups force students to develop strong teamwork skills and expose team members to the backgrounds and experience that each individual team member brings to the class.

Outside of class

MBA students work very hard and have schedules filled with both classes and activities. You could have the opportunity to play for an MBA sports team, work on a business plan competition, sit in on a talk by a famous CEO, or attend a social event with your classmates. Your out-of-class time would also be filled with studying, reading, and working on group projects.

Some MBA programs offer the opportunity to consult with real companies during the semester to truly integrate what you are learning in class with real-world scenarios, which may occur outside of normal class hours. Finally, keep in mind that the primary reason you would consider b-school is to advance your career. Therefore, a good portion of your time would also be devoted to networking for the purpose of finding career opportunities, working on your resume, and applying for internships and post-MBA jobs.

Final steps for success

If you apply and are accepted, what can you do to prepare to begin your MBA program? Here are some final steps for success:

- Warm up with basic finance and economics reading, and brush up on statistics and algebra (Kaplan's MBA Fundamentals series is a great start).
- If you don't already, begin reading business publications to stay abreast of current issues and trends that will come up in class.
- Talk to any current students or alumni of your program for thoughts and advice.

In the end, what will you truly get out of the MBA?

You will graduate with strong management, teamwork, and leadership skills. You will have taken a variety of courses on specific business disciplines, such as finance, marketing, strategy, operations, and more. You'll be forced to develop skills such as knowing what questions to ask, assessing the big picture, analyzing data, and prioritizing action steps. These skills will serve you well no matter what career path you choose.

You would have also gained in unexpected ways. For example, you would have stronger communication skills, you would see the value of a network, and you would in most cases, have made a group of lifelong friends and contacts who know you better than most people in your life, a benefit you may not have expected that will reward you for years to come.

To learn more about Kaplan's GMAT programs, please visit us online at www.kaptest. com/gmat